The Living Spirit

One Woman's Battle Amongst Ghosts, Spirits & The Living

Carole Bromley

ISBN 978 - 1479227358

First published 2009

Second Edition 2013

Acknowledgements

Special thanks to:

John J Williamson, (D.Sc), The Society of Metaphysicians, Hastings

Professor Ray J Paul, Professor Fay Weldon

Ron Bowers, Spiritual Photographer

Jackie Weaver, 'The Animal Psychic'

For my family of deceased furry friends

Becky, Bonnie, Magic, Lady

I love you always

This book I Dedicate To

My Mum, Dad & Sister in spirit to whom I love and thank for being part of my life

My Spirit Guide, Hannah

My husband Steve deserves the biggest thanks of all for the support and understanding he has given me. For all the love and care he has shared with me over the last 17 years at the time of writing this book. He has always been there for me, in sickness and in health.

I love you always

With love to my brothers Alan and Philip

Contents

Foreword

I first met Carole in early 2003, when I returned to my office as Dean of the Faculty of Technology and Information Systems, and there in the secretary's space in the office leading to mine was a temporary secretary. She was dressed somewhat unconventionally, which matched her every other activity. She continued to be different, declaring herself as a medium – and then demonstrating that she knows things about people that surprise them when she tells them. I held on to her as my secretary since I found she had an inner calm as well as excellent organisational skill. I have always taken the view that I should help people develop, and Carole appreciated that. I retired early in September of that year since I had Parkinson's disease.

I was retired but continued working in an honorary capacity, which was appreciated but difficult to utilise since my time keeping might be within days rather than minutes. It was agreed to provide me with some support and I went and got Carole back. So there I was, no job, no salary but a full-time secretary! What did she do? Some examples: Carole tried very hard to fix my going-home departure time by using her persuasive skills on my appointees to only spend so many minutes with me; she dealt with all the flack when I was not on time or did not turn up; car parking, taxi booking, negotiating appointments, helping people get help from me, sorting out my emails and correspondence and responding to many of them for me were all part of her every day remit. And many other activities, I am not that easy to work for!

When interviewed for the job she was asked, given the nature of academia with its prima donnas down to its angry students, how she would deal with the stress of the job. "I don't do stress" she calmly replied. Another example of her sense of humour is that when things are going wrong she announces she is "having a blonde day today".

Although I did not know what to make of her skills as a medium, I was sure she had some abilities beyond my comprehension, and since I know that what I do not know far exceeds my little knowledge, she came into the unknown region comfortably for me. We have worked together a little on this (see below) and I expect we will continue to do so.

I still do not know what to make of the Spirit World. During my illness there are many things that have happened to me for which we have no explanation. It is said that everything we know about what the brain does accounts for a quarter of its volume. So what does the rest do? With that level of knowledge about us, I believe it is wrong to assume that those people who have an unusual understanding of the world can be so casually written off as necessarily imposters or charlatans. Carole gives me challenges that make me think more about these things. So as we have discussed our views over time, this has led us to contemplating the writing of a debating book on the subject.

This brings me to this book, The Living Spirit, one woman's battle amongst ghosts, spirits and the living. Although I have known Carole for six years now, most of this book was revelatory to me. What stories, events, emotions – no fiction can match the story of Carole's sister, the abject fear and terror of her youth, the casual disdain from so called intelligent people, and at the end, having learnt to adjust, managing her talents to the benefit of mankind.

Something is going on out there and if you are curious about, this is a 'must-read' book. I challenge anyone to read this book, and then declare that it's all made up. My reaction to this would be the same as Keynes in the following story. When asked what he thought of the review by Hayek of Keynes' Treatise on Money, Keynes replied: "Hayek has not read my book with that measure of 'good will' which an author is entitled to expect of a reader. Until he does so he will not know what I mean or whether I am right".

If you wish to disbelieve this book, you will succeed. If you have an open mind, this book will make you think. I am still thinking!

Professor Ray J Paul, Author of *Living with Parkinson's Disease: Shake, Rattle and Roll.*

Introduction

The 'dead' have mostly always haunted me, or have I haunted them? Do they haunt you? You know how a living person can haunt you by always being there, sometimes getting on your nerves, that's how I found the 'dead', always there, always around me, far from getting on my nerves, more like creating my nerves! It wasn't always nice either, well, not in the beginning.

But, here we both are, you interested in ghosts and me telling you about them; like me, you want to know more. You've either got one, want one, or want to get rid of one, either way, you're interest in ghosts is just as inquisitive as mine, but just *how* inquisitive are you? You can decide for yourself, one way or another, but the choice is *not* only yours. For many, the encounter of a ghost is a bit like a blind date, neither of you has met one another, or even knows one another. For others, an encounter with a ghost is most probably someone you know.

With so much public and media attention, a ghost is becoming increasingly more of a 'must have' household commodity than ever before. The thought of being 'haunted' can be a 'haunting' thought in itself. Even the prospect of not being 'haunted' when you want to be 'haunted' can be something that we may want, but can't have. Admit it, you either love or hate the concept of having, or not having a ghostly presence in your home. But, since there are so many ghosts out there, a home is sometimes not a home without at least one haunting.

These 'must have' commodities come with a range of negative and positive personalities, strengths and freewill. These 'commodities' are available anywhere and everywhere believe it or not. But, going down to your local supermarket and selecting one straight off the shelf and popping it into your shopping trolley just isn't going to happen. It's not because there is any shortage you'll be pleased to know, since the supply of ghosts is limitless.

But, why on earth would someone want a ghost if they don't know what to do with one? It's not like you can lock it in a room and expect it to stay there till you get back, or think you can take it with you everywhere you go, contrary to what some may believe. A ghost is transparent and non-physical and has the ability to walk through doors, wood or physical matter and is a non human talent.

Let's face it; nothing can be more intriguing or fascinating than someone down the local pub, or sitting next to you on a train journey telling you about their own encounters with a ghost. Current trends such as TV, magazines and national newspapers indicate the 'dead' are becoming a more popular topic of conversation.

Even more fascinating is that same someone often telling you who they believe their ghost to be. Naturally, they will tell you the ghost is probably that of one of their late grandparents, a parent, brother, son, daughter, close friend and so on. The reality is, people tell you what they want you to believe, what they want to believe too.

When someone tells me they have a ghost but have no idea who it is, I know I should worry. I should worry because they have told me about it, which means they are worrying. But, whether it's a family ghost, or the ghost of a friend, how would you know who it really was? Unless you could communicate with it that is.

Imagine for one moment your gut feeling tells you that the ghost is not who you believe it to be, how would that make you feel? Haunted? Yes, of course it would. Imagine then if you felt you knew the ghost was someone you loved, would you still feel haunted? Yes, of course you would. But, would it make you feel better convincing yourself that the ghost you feel with you is that of a friend or loved one? Probably - but then again, probably not.

I say you'd probably feel better because we can have a deep yearning not to let go of those we knew, loved and still love. We have a yearning to keep our loved ones close to our heart and our mind. We know when our loved ones are close when strange things that cannot be explained start to happen. It takes some getting used to knowing that you are being visited from beyond the grave. Whether we know who we are being visited by or not, we still react to that of which we are unsure. Do we really want to know who is visiting us? Does it really matter to us?

Believe it or not, there are people out there who really want a ghost in their own home, no matter if the ghost is a member of the family or a friend. I've known people who would accept any ghost going, as long as it was a ghost walking amongst them in their own home. And of course, there are those who don't want any ghostly visitors at all. But, do we have the choice of inviting ghosts into our homes or not? Do we have a choice what type of ghost we want in our home? Do we even know if we have visitors from the other side? Maybe, maybe not!

The 'dead' haunt me and I haunt them. Seeing, hearing, touching, feeling, smelling and talking to the 'dead' are all a normal and natural daily phenomena for me. I have come to accept through years of experience, and through no fault of my own the 'dead' can communicate. I am part of the majority who don't believe we *die* or become *'dead'*. Besides, from my experience and knowledge, there's far too much going on in the afterlife that keeps me busy as a psychic medium and paranormal research investigator.

Yet, I didn't start out in this life as a psychic or a medium, but rather grew into it, or it grew into me because the 'dead' contact me. It's because of my conversations with the 'dead' that I had a need to understand them more. I had a need to understand the living too. I found myself trapped between two dimensions in listening and talking to the 'dead' and defending myself against the living. This is my story, 'one woman's battle amongst 'ghosts', 'spirits' and the 'living'.

When I talk of *spirit* or *spirits* it is with the understanding that a deceased person or persons from the spirit world are making a communication with me. It may not refer to any particular spirit in general, but to spirit itself.

Broadly speaking, I had been thrown into the deep end by spirit and I was made to either sink or swim. I'm good at sinking. I drowned when I found things always went on in middle of the night, or when it was dark. I was terrified of the dark, not something many people would openly admit to. It takes some getting used to, being alone in the dark, especially when you know you're not alone. Now my fear of the dark has diminished and I am no longer afraid. I am no longer afraid of the 'dead' either, but the 'living' can be spooky!

This book is based on events with actual ghosts, spirits and the living. It offers the truth, the whole truth and nothing but truth. Never before had I experienced so many battles and confrontations with ghosts in my house. Never before had I been frightened and tormented by their presence. They were taking over my life. I was afraid of my own house, I was afraid to live in my own home. I couldn't hide or move away because the ghosts would always be there; they would let me know they were with me. The whispering of voices never stopped. Living with fear isn't easy.

Spirit started to take a great interest in me and became part of my life from when I was six years old. I had not got an imaginary friend, I had a ghost. At the age of eleven and on New Year's Eve 1970, I heard voices predicting my own sister's tragic death. These voices would haunt me for many years, voices that still haunt me to this day. The 'dead' would show up anytime and anywhere to talk to me, I had no control. The 'dead' believed in me, I had a duty to believe in them. I had to learn how to work with them.

I was to learn how to work with my spirit guide, Hannah, who eventually taught me how to work with other spirits, but not through a crash course! I hadn't realised Hannah had been with me for most of life, nor had I realised it was her voice that would always be whispering to me. Of course, there would be other voices talking to me too. Some I knew, some I didn't, some I would have rather not known.

Knowing that spirit (returning memories of a deceased person), and ghosts (earth bound spirits of a deceased person) exist led me to conduct my own investigations. Investigating haunted places and being aware of the unknown (spirit), and the known (living), proved to be quite a battle. I never knew what to expect. It would be frightening at first, visiting haunted places and organising teams of people to work with one another, I had a fear of both! However, the spirits were easy to work with once I had confronted my fear. It was the same fear I had when I used to confront the ghosts in my house. Telling spirit to behave was something I became accustomed to doing. Telling the 'living' to behave was another matter!

I learnt many lessons, one of them was to learn that our deceased loved ones still exist and that death is a human myth. There is no death, but if you want to think you die and that's it, then that's your prerogative. If you want to believe there is more to life than the one you live now then that's your future.

Every day is a future and battle for those who are of a spiritual mind. Every day I realise how the belief of Spiritualism can be exploited for the purpose of designer science, media propaganda and entertainment. I conducted my own research and investigated if science, after hundreds of years has managed to prove or disprove the theory of an afterlife. Since science is not a religion it will never serve any part of my belief system. Science and Spiritualism are two separate belief systems. They should not be forced upon one another where representation of evidence of the soul's survival can be grossly misunderstood.

This is my story, a woman confronting her fears of the 'dead', and the 'living'. This is my story of a spiritual journey where I grew up in two worlds, one of physical matter, one of transparency. I am the woman who is going to take you on an incredible journey of fear and discovery. I am the woman who is going to reveal and expose a personal and intimate part of her life to you. I want you to hear and share with me the voices I have heard; I want you to feel the ghosts and spirits who stand beside you as they have stood beside me. Thank you for allowing me to share my story with you.

Psychic Child

My very first ghost made an appearance when I was a shy little six-year old child. The ghost wasn't alone, he had others with him. The others I couldn't see but I would always hear them. I lived in a council house in Manchester with my mum, dad, two older brothers, older sister and twin brother. It was just my luck a ghost appeared when I was on my own. It couldn't choose to show up in front of any of my three other brothers, or my sister, no sir, it had to be tiny tots little me. Me, who knew absolutely nothing about ghosts or the living 'dead'. Why should I know about the 'dead'?

I thought everyone could see the 'dead' in the same way I did. I thought everyone could hear the voices too, but they didn't. I didn't know I wasn't 'normal', but then I thought nor was anyone else. No one else could see or hear the same phenomenon as me. I didn't even know what a ghost was since I thought they were the same as any human being.

Mum had kept me away from school because I was poorly. It was a rainy day where the clash of thunder made a terrifying noise. I always knew when the thunder would come because bolts of lightning would flash across the sky. I was scared, I didn't like the electric storm and it wouldn't go away. Mum was ok though, she didn't seem to mind what was going on outside with the weather. She was busy in the back room ploughing through the baskets of clothes that needed ironing. It seemed she was always ironing. She would stand for long hours behind the ironing board, laboriously pressing the hot iron across the never ending pile of clothes. Mum was very maternal and always took good care of her children, especially when one of us was ill. She would always be there to love and hug us. She would always make us feel better, no matter how tired she felt.

Mum did think I had a good imagination for a kid of my age though. There were many times when she didn't know what to think of me. There were times when I didn't know what to think of her too. I could see and hear things she couldn't, I could see and hear things no one else could. I couldn't figure out why. Because I was poorly and off school I had been confined to the sofa, I was restless. I was on the sofa because it saved mum keep putting the iron down when she needed to check on me. It also saved her many trips from running up and down the stairs countless times. I didn't want to lie on the sofa though, it was boring. I was bored and mum was busy. I needed something to do.

Throwing the blanket on the floor mum had tucked over me earlier I stood up on the sofa watching the rain as it hit hard against the windows. The electrical storm zapping over the rooftops of the houses began to get closer to our house. The sound of the thunder was getting closer, it scared me. I was scared in case the lightning hit our house. I would duck down from the window every time the flash of lighting came close. I didn't want it to hurt me.

I was happy-ish standing at the window keeping my eye on the weather. Except now the weather was not the only thing I found myself looking at. In the street and in the pouring rain was a clown waving to me. I watched as the clown danced up and down outside our house, he was smiling and waving at me with big open arms. He looked like he was beckoning me to go outside and join him in the street.

I wasn't interested in the clown's silly antics and shook my head as though I was acknowledging a 'No, you're not funny.' I was doing one of those pathetic long and noisy sobs kids do when they're not happy. I must have gone on a bit too long because I could no longer see the clown, he wasn't outside. This irritated me, but not for long. The clown walked through the living room door. I stopped crying and found myself unable to move from the sofa. He had my attention; I never knew people could walk through closed doors!

He was laughing as he walked backwards and forwards in and out of the living room walls. I was laughing with him, at least until I tried to walk through the wall myself and bashed my head in the process. Well, I was trying to copy him. I bashed my head so hard it made me scream out with pain. The clown made it look very easy and very natural to walk through solid matter.

On hearing my screams mum came rushing in and saw me holding my head. She picked me up and hurried me into the kitchen. Flinging open the fridge door she grabbed a tub of margarine off the shelf. Before I knew what she was going to do with it she had slapped a dollop of the stuff on the now rising bump on my head. The margarine was supposedly used to make the swelling go down, although why people used margarine in those days was a mystery. Nor can I remember if it actually made me feel any better.

Tantrums and tears over, Mum returned me to the sofa and lay me down; I needed a rest after all the screaming and crying I had done. Yet, I wanted to see the clown again but he had gone. I was trying to explain to Mum how I came to bump my head. I was trying to explain between each sob how I wanted the clown to come back. Mum didn't know what to make of my garbled nonsense about the clown, she was puzzled. Nevertheless, she promised to get me a clown next time we were at the local market. She kept her promise; I did get a clown but not one that walked through walls, or one that made me smile. The meeting with the clown was to be my first experience of countless visits from the other side. I didn't know that meeting was with such a thing as a 'ghost'.

Even though I did not see the clown again it didn't stop the voices I heard. Voices I thought were 'normal.' I would hear voices whispering behind the door at bed time. I'd call out to Mum or Dad but there would be no answer. I'd get up and look outside the door, but there would be no one there. I would sneak downstairs looking for Mum, Dad, or anyone who I thought could be doing the talking.

Sulking, I would ask Mum why she or Dad didn't answer me when I called. Mum would claim no one had been upstairs and tell me to go back to bed. I thought they were playing tricks on me. I always thought people were playing tricks on me when I heard voices and no one was there.

I wouldn't go back up the stairs on my own; mum would have to come with me. Before I went to bed I would ask Mum to check my bedroom. I would ask her to check the cupboards and under the bed. I wouldn't go into the room unless she had checked it and I had seen her do it. I always believed 'others', whoever they were lived among us. These 'others' I thought were normal, only they weren't, were they?

It was always comforting as a child having someone around besides my 'living' family, although I didn't see anyone else except the clown. It didn't stop me from hearing the whispering of voices. When I played with my dolls I would hear someone talking behind me, only there was no one there. There were times when I'd get annoyed with the voices and tell them to 'shut up'. I was sad but glad when my parents decided to move south to London.

I was eight years old when we moved to our new house. The new house we had moved into did not speak to me at first. I missed the voices. The voices were no longer there, my invisible friends had gone. I had got used to living without them until three years later when the whispering started again. I cannot explain for the life of me why they disappeared for three years. Perhaps it was because my parents were getting a divorce.

The house had to be sold and our family split up. Mum took me and my brother to a house that was better known as sheltered housing. It was a large dark and sombre looking house which we shared with other single mums and their children. I hated it. We had one room and one bed which the three of us slept in. It was horrible, the family being split up. Mum had little money for us all to make the train and bus journeys to see my brothers and sister. They had been fortunate to live with other family members. Mum managed her best to keep us as a family and would keep us together whenever she could. It wasn't easy. My childhood wasn't easy, but it was happy. We may not have had much, but at least we had love.

We would have to get up early to make the train and bus journeys to school. Mum always made sure we were never late. We always looked clean and tidy; Mum wouldn't have anyone tell her that her kids were dirty and unkempt! She wasn't frightened of work either, and took on jobs to make ends meet. The work didn't pay well but at least she felt she was able to provide for us.

After we had lived in sheltered housing for almost a year, the Council allocated Mum a proper house. We could be together again as a family, except dad wouldn't be there. It was quite a strange house really compared to the one mum and dad had previously owned. It was strange because there was no bathroom. The bath we had was in the small kitchen next to the large Butler kitchen sink. It was covered with two heavy boards that would be lifted off when it was bath time. Saucepans and kettles would have to be put on the gas stove to fill the bath with hot water. At bath times we all got in each other's water, it was cheaper. We wouldn't be allowed to go in the kitchen if someone was in the bath.

So, if we needed to go to the toilet at bath time we would have to go out the front door, walk to the bottom of the road, through an alleyway till we reached our back garden and the outside toilet. Of course, the toilet was just another feature of this undersized family house we found ourselves in. If we needed a visit to the toilet at night Mum would tell us we couldn't. It was too dark, the house backed onto a recreation field. Besides, sometimes the weather wouldn't allow, which meant we would have to use a bucket placed in the corner of the bedroom.

At teatime we all perched our plates on our laps. We ate in the living room adjacent to the kitchen. We had no dining table; there wasn't enough room in the one tiny sitting room we had to cramp into. It made it very awkward for Mum to cook for us all; meals always got cold waiting for the next one to arrive. We did have three bedrooms though which was a blessing. My two brothers slept in one room in the same bed. My sister who was eighteen years old was the only one with her own room. Me and my twin brother shared Mum's bed, my brother would be sleeping one side of her and I the other. We couldn't have been a closer family if we tried!

Even the neighbours were like part of our extended family. When Mum took me to visit the old ladies, or the 'grannies' as I used to refer to them, they were always nice to me. They always treated me like they were my own Gran. The houses down our street always seemed to be occupied by widows whose husband's had died before them. Mum would visit them every day to do their shopping and odd jobs. She always made sure the elderly ladies were looked after. She had a heart of gold mum did, always thinking about the welfare and well-being of others before herself.

Nothing was too much trouble for mum, despite five kids she always managed to find time for the elderly. Whilst she was at the shops I would get up to no good with the granny I had been left behind with to chat to. I was always entertained when they brought out their tin of old photographs. I used to sit and amuse them by talking about people in the photos they were showing me. The voices would be talking to me as I'd tell them people's names that were already deceased and often be right. I would also get a telling off from Mum for making up 'stories.' The grannies used to tell her I was telling the truth!

Mum used to think I was scaring the 'grannies' by talking about their deceased loved ones, but I believed I was really scaring her. She didn't like me talking about the 'dead' and I didn't understand why. I didn't want to believe that once people were gone they were gone, finito; burnt at the crematorium or buried in a church yard. I knew more than Mum did about the 'dead' but she wouldn't listen to me. To me the 'dead' were living.

Sometimes the 'grannies' would ask if I had a dad. I would tell them my Mum and Dad didn't live together any more. Sometimes, I'm sure they were being nosey when they kept asking questions about Dad. I never felt comfortable talking about dad, mostly because mum didn't like me to. Nonetheless, Christmas wasn't the same without both my parents in the house at the same time. It seemed unfair because all the other kids had a mum and dad for Christmas, but me, I only had my mum. It didn't matter though that Mum was the only parent I had, well not really since our family was close.

Our closeness as a family would change when I reached eleven years old, our family would be torn apart. It was New Years Eve 1970; my family were getting ready to go out celebrating. My sister Christine had got engaged to Colin but we were also celebrating my brother and his wife's birth of their first new born baby two days earlier. It was also a night I was to experience the strongest voice of spirit I had ever heard. This voice was loud and firm, it wasn't a whisper.

17

My twin brother and I were to stay at home with a neighbour friend of Mum's; she would pop in now and again to check on us. It was safe to leave kids alone in the house in those days. The community was safe and friendly; everyone knew one another too so helping neighbours out would be no problem. People were happy to have good neighbours.

I was happy for my family as I stood in the middle of the small front room watching everyone fall over one another in their haste to get ready. I was falling over as I tried to dodge out of the way. I was looking and laughing at my sister who was proudly showing off her engagement ring to us all. I loved my sister to bits but alarm bells rang when I thought I heard a voice whisper in my ear, 'Say goodbye to your sister she's not coming back.' I ignored the voice. We were all excited about the engagement and the birth of our first grandchild, my nephew. We had good reasons to celebrate.

I was jumping up and down smiling at Christine asking if I could try her ring on when I heard the voice again very clearly. It repeated the words, 'Say goodbye to your sister, you won't see her again.' I couldn't understand who was talking to me because I couldn't see anyone who was talking to me; besides who would say such a thing? I asked my sister Christine if she was coming back after her night out and she replied, 'Yes, of course I am silly.' Feeling relieved I smiled at her and thought no more of the voice. I put it down to my imagination, but I had my doubts, it felt real, someone was talking to me. I knew it wasn't my imagination.

Everyone in the family set off out, my mother, sister and her new fiancé, my two brothers and their girlfriends, leaving me and my twin brother watching TV on the sofa. Even though Dad was no longer living with us it was still crowded with the six of us living in such a small house.

Our closeness as a family was to be destroyed by the double tragedy of my sister and her fiancé. Those voices I had heard earlier were haunting me. I was sure someone other than my family was in the house, but if there was I couldn't find them. As much as I tried I couldn't forget the voice telling me 'Say goodbye to your sister, you won't see her again.' I didn't like the voice.

After everyone had said their goodbyes my brother and I settled down on the settee watching TV. We had a black and white telly that needed feeding with shillings through the slot meter fixed to the back. The telly was off more than it was on, Mum couldn't afford to run it every day. However, Christmas was a treat in our house and Mum always made sure we had enough pennies to watch telly over the holiday.

My brother fell asleep with me sitting next to him; I was glued to the telly but couldn't stop thinking about the voice. It was during the thoughts about the voice that I had the fright of my life. I'm sure if I was a cat I would have used nine lives with the amount of frights I was to endure. Panic stricken, my eyes followed the ornaments that were on the fireplace rising up into the air. I knew this was not normal, nor was the grey mist that formed around them. The ornaments on the telly started to float in mid air before settling back down again. This was not normal either. Nor was the putrid odour that filled the room, it was a smell I couldn't explain.

I shook my brother trying to wake him up but he remained in a good state of sleep. I was frightened at what I was seeing. Shaking him hard I shouted at him to wake up. When he finally stirred I told him of what I had witnessed. He wasn't bothered and went back to sleep. It wasn't long after he dozed back off that there was a banging on the window. Something else that wasn't normal. I shook my brother again and shouted at him 'someone's banging on the window'. This time he heard it and we both froze, we sat there looking at one another as the banging on the window continued. I told him to go see who it was but he was just as reluctant as me.

After a bit of a debate my brother finally went to the window, I was right behind him. Pulling back the curtain he saw the figure of a policeman peering back at him through the window. He was pointing at the door. We opened the door to the policeman who looked cold and covered in snow. It had been a magical Christmas with the snow falling. We were asked if our parents were home as he needed to speak to them. We explained to him everyone was out but he could find mum down at one of the local clubs. The policeman had come to deliver an urgent message but would not tell us what it was. Whatever it was I didn't feel it was going to be good.

I was going to mention about what I had seen happening earlier with the ornaments but thought better of it. I didn't want to mention the voices either. I never spoke of what had happened to anyone. I thought it was a bad thing I had heard and seen so didn't want to talk about it, kept it to myself. It was bad enough feeling something was wrong without someone telling me I was 'imagining' it. I didn't want anyone telling me I had made up any unbelievable story.

Mum and the family soon returned home but I just knew something was wrong. I thought the worst because of the voices I had heard. Something was terribly wrong though; my older brother took me and my twin brother upstairs. Mum was crying and hysterical, I didn't know what on earth could be the matter. I was crying for her, we were all crying.

My older brother sat us down on my sister's bed and told us Christine wasn't coming home, or ever coming back again. He told us she was alright but we wouldn't see her again, she wasn't coming home. With tears in his eyes he told us she had died in a tragic car accident with her fiancé. They had both died together. I thought she wasn't alright; she couldn't be alright if she wasn't coming back. That didn't seem alright to me. My sister and her fiancé were both only eighteen years old. They had gone out with their friends when their car had skidded, crashed then ended up wrapped round a tree.

The driver had been intoxicated with alcohol whilst at the wheel of the car. He and his partner were very fortunate and survived the fatality. The driver was fined for taking two people's lives. He had destroyed the lives of two families left to pick up the pieces. His punishment is enough; he will live with the tragedy for the rest of his life. Yet, in my eyes, we were the ones being punished. I had no sister anymore, my mum and dad had lost a daughter, my brothers had lost their sister. My sister would never have children, nor would she be the mother she had always dreamed of being. Our lives would be empty.

I cried and cried blaming myself for her death. I blamed myself for the voices I thought were my own. I blamed myself for the voices I heard speaking to me. I somehow felt responsible that I had my own sister, whom I loved and adored taken away from me and my family.

Of course, I didn't tell anyone about the voices I had heard before she died. I was an eleven year old kid, who would believe me? It was my secret because I didn't want to get into trouble. The memory of the voices will never leave me, they haunt me. I hear them clearly as though it was only yesterday. It seems like a memory, but a memory can last forever. Forever seems like torture.

My sister and I were identical in looks; people would often mix us up or get our names mixed up. Even after she died people would call me by her name, even my own doctor! For years I didn't understand the voices. On reaching the age of eighteen I thought it would be my turn to die too, just as my sister had died. I was so relieved after I had reached the age of eighteen and was still living.

Haunted

We moved twice more following the death of my sister. At the age of twelve we moved to a house close to my secondary school. Mum didn't like to stay at the old house; it brought back too many memories. I think I was about fourteen when mum married again, she was happy. The happiness didn't last long because we would have to move to another house. Unfortunately, Jack, Mum's second husband had lung cancer and the house was not suitable for his needs. Another house and another home. I was glad I got to keep this one, but not without a battle. It was our seventh home. I was in no hurry to move out soon. I had seen my teen years through in house number seven.

I never actually left home for too long when I did leave home. Even when I married it wasn't long before me and Hubby (my husband), moved back in with mum. Happily married and still living with mum I should have had no worries. If it weren't for my sister's death I may have been able to settle. I couldn't settle, the voices kept haunting me. I was looking for answers and wanted to learn more about the 'dead'.

I was able to learn more through a programme on television where a medium stood in front of an audience of people giving messages. The messages he gave were coming from the 'dead', at the same time, demonstrating to those who received the messages their loved ones weren't 'dead'. I was fascinated and had to learn more. It was a good start for me in knowing there were 'others' like me out there.

The medium had a website and a forum where I could read messages posted by others, I could learn from him and others like him. Mostly, people spoke of their spirit guide, but I thought people had to be really special to have a guide. I wasn't special so didn't think I had one. I didn't think I deserved one because I had done nothing to deserve one.

The medium later installed a chat room on his website which I would visit nightly for many months. It was my presence in this chat room that enhanced my sense of clairaudience (psychic sense of clear hearing).

Through my nightly visitations at the internet chat room I felt 'others' with me. I could hear voices talking to me when no one was there. I would find myself typing information related to people's 'dead' relatives, or things connected to their past, present and future. I didn't have a clue as to why I could do this. I only knew I could do it because the voices told me what to say.

As the months went by I did meet Hannah, my spirit guide, she introduced herself to me in a dream. The dream was so real I almost felt being part of it but glad I wasn't. Hannah was working as a nurse in the Crimean war. I awoke from the dream when I heard someone call my name. It was Hannah, My spirit guide introducing herself to me.

I had not seen Hannah show herself to me in a physical form though which didn't really bother me. Neither did I know her name for almost the two years I had been working with her. Knowing her name wasn't important, at least that's what people kept telling me, and why should it?

It was good, I had met my spirit guide at long last, but I didn't have the experience to work with her. She was there and ready for me when eventually I figured out how the whole spiritual thing worked.

My inexperience of all things spiritual was something I wasn't prepared for. The more psychic readings I gave in the internet psychic chat room, the more strange things began to happen in my house. Things I couldn't explain. I was convinced our house was haunted and ghosts were lurking in every corner of the room. I was convinced someone was watching me, the 'ghosts' were watching me. I would feel a presence as a coldness came close to me. Sometimes I would smell a waft of tobacco, perfume, or the smell of death. The same smell that was present when my sister had died. I know the ghosts and spirits of the 'dead' wanted me to be aware of them, as they were aware of me.

There was no doubt in my mind how much aware of me the ghosts and spirits were. It didn't matter what time of day or night it was I knew I was never alone. There would always be a strange feeling in my house. It was funny how I would often think daytimes were good because of the natural light, but in reality daylight made no difference. There was no relevance as to when the 'dead' would visit. I knew my house was haunted and that I was being haunted. I knew the 'dead' were there, I just didn't know who the 'dead' were.

When I went to bed I knew it would be a living hell as soon as the lights went out. The 'dead' would be ever present. I'm not one to scare easily but I did live in fear. I feared I was being haunted by the 'dead' and by ghosts of the 'dead'. I had begun to see ghostly apparitions appear out of nothing and out of nowhere. At first it was nothing much, just bits of mist floating around in the room. All the same, I couldn't accept something more than hearing voices was happening. I didn't want to accept anything more than a voice.

I know in the past the odd one or two materialisations of a 'dead' person had presented itself to me. But, as the appearances were few and far between it didn't really bother me, it bothered me having them in my house. It shouldn't have made any difference but it did.

I had got used to someone talking to me and not knowing who it was. Nevertheless, it was always a one way conversation. Someone doing the talking and me doing the listening. How could I converse with someone I couldn't see? I couldn't, not really. I couldn't say it was Hannah, my Spirit guide all the time because the voices were never the same. Yet, most of my life a voice had been with me and I felt comfortable with that. I also knew a voice couldn't hurt me. My main concern was if a ghost could hurt me, I wasn't sure, but would soon find out since there seemed to be plenty more of them to come.

It was becoming obvious, ghosts and spirits were taking it upon themselves to move in and share my house with me. A house that was an ordinary ex-council house that shouldn't have been haunted, or so I thought. My house was situated in an ordinary street where ordinary people lived. I lived in my house with my husband, and Mum, both who were completely oblivious to the hauntings that were taking place.

Being 'haunted' I guess is not everyone's cup of tea, it certainly wasn't mine. Yet there is always a reason for everything, as I was to discover. It would be true to say that not everyone is aware they may have a ghost living with them. It would be reasonable to say that not everyone is even aware they are 'haunted.' Even if you do think you are haunted, who do you try to convince, yourself or others? More importantly, who would believe you?

The prospect of my house being haunted is something I knew my husband and my mum would find hard to believe. I couldn't talk to Mum about ghosts because it spooked her, she believed in letting the 'dead' rest in peace. I believed that the 'dead' sometimes didn't want to rest in peace; I knew they were very much still 'alive.' I couldn't tell hubby either we had ghosts; he was a sceptic and would laugh at me. Worse still, divorce me!

Mum was unfortunate to grow up in a society where one shouldn't speak of the dead, or speak to the 'dead.' I was always careful and discreet not to frighten her by talking about the 'dead.' I never spoke of the activities that were going on, especially when she was sleeping. I was happy to know how well she did sleep!

Having a good undisturbed night's sleep was something that became impossible for me. I didn't want to go to sleep. It became increasingly difficult to sleep anyway with the amount of ghostly activity going on. When darkness came my bedroom developed its own heart beat and came alive. It had a mind of its own, but only I could hear it living and breathing.

I found myself living and breathing amongst the living and the 'dead', except I didn't know much about the 'dead', or ghosts, or even that they were real. I didn't want the 'dead' to exist in my world, but they did. Yes, I wanted them to exist metaphorically speaking, but in their own world, not mine.

I became aware that ghosts appeared to be more active at night, well, in my house they did. I was also aware that my own psychic senses were rapidly developing and that I was becoming more 'aware'. I had begun to see what appeared to be the outlines of people appear. I didn't like what I saw and went into denial. I feared the 'ghosts' would be lurking behind the doors, in the wardrobes or behind the curtains, perhaps under the bed, or even in it. I knew the 'ghosts' were always there … somewhere.

I would find myself sweating and shaking with fear, especially at bedtime but I wasn't ill, since there was nothing physically or mentally wrong with me. I just didn't want to go to bed, or be in my bedroom. It was mostly there the constant visitations from ghosts of the 'dead' would appear.

Apparitions, ghosts and the 'dead' were people I would rather not see. Well, ghosts were apparitions of the 'dead' after all. My lamp stayed on when Hubby was working a night shift. I didn't like the dark or what moved within the dark. I kept my bedside lamp light on so I couldn't see them. I didn't want to see them, but I knew they could see me.

It was during one night when I became obsessed, (not possessed) with a feeling of being watched. I could sense someone's presence. I could sense someone's eyes looking at me from each corner of the room. Someone's eyes peering down at me from the bedroom ceiling watching over me. It was a bit like when someone stands behind you and you're aware of a presence, but you don't know who that presence is. That's how it was for me, aware someone was with me, and me living with the 'unknown.

The 'unknown' became part of me, as did not knowing who was with me. It felt rather intrusive at times. There were times when I could feel the energies around me distinctly change. I would feel someone breathing down my neck, or feel the wisp of a breath cross my face. I even used to feel someone touching me on the shoulder, head, hand or arm. I would feel my heart beat faster with fear as I sensed a presence close to me. Goose bumps would form on my arms whenever the thought crossed my mind of a 'dead' person close to me.

Seeing the 'dead' didn't happen overnight, but gradually over a long period of time. I didn't ask to see the 'dead', nor did I want to see 'dead' people. I didn't want to particularly see the 'dead' materialise in front of me either. It was probably easy for them to accept me; it was harder for me to accept them. Their visitations didn't please me; they often appeared at night, in my bedroom, whether I was alone or not, I could feel them.

I got to the stage where I could no longer be in my bedroom on my own, or any other room for that matter. I got into a routine where I would only go to bed if Hubby was going. If he was on a night shift I would have to face the prospect of being on my own. I would be on my own with the 'dead' for the night. If he was home I would always make sure he was in the bedroom before me. If he went to the bathroom then little old me would tag along to the bathroom with him. He must have thought I was madly in love with him following him around everywhere, or perhaps raving bonkers! Well, I wasn't bonkers, but of course I loved him and wanted to be 'closer' to him, perhaps more than he would have liked, I became his shadow!

I did my best in trying not to be noticed by the ghosts, silly I know but it's something a person *would* attempt to do. However, before bedtime I would have to visit the bathroom as my last port of call for the night. I didn't like to hang around in this room for too long in case a ghost appeared. My make-up stayed fixed to my face quite often because I couldn't bear to be alone in the bathroom. Failure to remove my make-up before bedtime resulted in something similar to a Picasso on the pillowcase. As for my face, well, that had similarities to an artist's palette on a bad day!

It wasn't just my make-up I neglected; I'd also notice how my clothes were placed in no particular order spread across the bedroom floor. Opening the wardrobe doors and hanging my clothes up was something I couldn't do. I was always afraid of what, or who was lurking inside.

After my clothes fell crumpled on the floor I would dive into bed grabbing hold of the duvet and hide safely underneath it. I would pull the duvet over me, peering over the top only if I felt brave enough to see what was going on outside. I knew I never imagined anything I saw, nor did I question what I did see since I knew I didn't need to.

I felt like a kid playing hide 'n' seek only I was doing the hiding. I couldn't breathe under the duvet but it made me feel safe. The duvet was my protection. Ha! Ha! Protection from what, or worse still ... who? Coming up for air from under the duvet was a necessity, whether I liked it or not. Of course, I would only appear with my eyes closed just in case I saw something, or someone.

I didn't feel any room in my house was really safe except for the bathroom, not that I liked being there either. The bathroom had a lock on it and would keep the 'ghosts' out, or so I thought, silly me. Locking doors would not keep ghosts out because 'ghosts' can walk through solid matter. This function had already been proved with the clown. Nonetheless, locking it made me feel safe.

There would be no escape, locked doors or not, it didn't matter. There would always be the sighting of mysterious black shadows. Shadows moving swiftly across the top of the stairs became a regular event. As the shadows moved the lights would flicker and the floor boards creak. This bothered me as I couldn't lock the shadows out either.

I was never too eager to visit the bathroom. If you saw what I saw, you too would think the same about visiting your bathroom, or other rooms for that matter. However, one night I reluctantly plucked up the courage to go it alone and make a visit. It was much to my annoyance that I hadn't gone sooner.

A visit to the bathroom was becoming not so much of a convenience, but an inconvenience. It was during one of Hubby's night shifts an inconvenience occurred and I couldn't wait till he came home, or until daylight broke. Cursing under my breath I made a dash for the toilet and the bathroom. I was wishing I had gone sooner. I was trying to function very quickly, but how do you hurry a pee! I hated every minute of this unplanned short visit. I hated the prospect that someone may be watching me. Not a nice thought, but we can think like that can't we, someone watching us.

I sat there on the edge of the toilet checking the room making sure I was alone. I glanced at the windowsill where a small mirror sat on the tiled ledge. The mirror began to bother me the more I looked at it. It was strange how something drew my attention to glance up behind me towards the mirror. Why on earth I would want to look in the mirror when all I would expect to see was a reflection of the shower curtain I'll never know. But, this particular night I did and wished I hadn't.

How I wished I hadn't looked up. Staring straight back at me in the mirror was my face clear as crystal. It wouldn't have been weird except I was looking at least 10 years younger! Shouldn't complain I know; anything that makes any woman look a year younger let alone 10 is a blessing! I stuttered as I yelled out 'heck', or words to that affect. What I was witnessing was not my imagination, nor was it physically possible or plausible. If it wasn't for the mid flow pee I'd have legged it back to bed. But since I couldn't stop, having to up knickers and run was not an option. As I sat there miserably looking directly in front of me, to the side of me, but not behind me, I was telling myself to hurry up. This pee went on and on.

I didn't think this funny at all, I was not amused. It didn't make sense and I certainly didn't hang about for the luxury of a wipe or to wash my hands. I legged it straight back to bed throwing my duvet angrily over my head. I shook with fear as I closed my eyes.

I was breathing fast, my heart was beating rapidly. I was in shock. I could feel my throat tighten as my body perspired with fear. The room temperature had changed and I began to feel intensely cold. The dead quiet and stillness of the night made it feel very eerie. I didn't like it. I made a point of leaving my bedside lamp switched on. It was a touch lamp that got brighter or darker, depending how many times you touched it. I never turned out the light if I was on my own, but it didn't stop the 'ghosts' from turning it on, or off.

The lamp would play games with me; it was like it had a mind of its own sometimes. I was glad the lamp was on though as I didn't want to see any ghosts or shadows. Normal people turn lights on so they can see things; I would turn my lights on so I couldn't see things. I used to think by having my lamp switched on the 'ghosts' wouldn't show up and I wouldn't see them. I didn't particularly want to see the 'dead', ghosts, apparitions, or shadows in the light or dark.

I felt safe curled up in bed with the light on. I would stretch out my limbs now and again just to change position. I did this quietly as I didn't want to disturb anyone outside the bed, or let it be known to anyone I was awake. I wasn't good at pretending to be asleep! Popping my head out from under the duvet once in a while I would check the room. I would check the room like I was on guard duty. My eyes would search the walls, ceiling, curtains, TV, four corners of the room, door and furniture for any sighting of a ghost. I couldn't relax but at least if I didn't see anything I could feel relieved, relief was good!

In bed I made sure I was motionless and entwined in the protection of my duvet, not wanting to move, not daring to move in case anyone saw me or heard me. Who was I kidding? There was only my mum in the house when Hubby was working and she wouldn't disturb me. Only I wasn't talking about the physical here, I was talking about the non-physical, ghosts of the 'dead'.

I lay in my bed for what seemed like hours, when in reality only an hour had passed when I heard a voice whisper to me. I heard a voice as it whispered, 'Look behind you.' Not really having a nervous breakdown or anything my lips were trembling as I mumbled to myself, 'Who said that.' I knew my sense of hearing was good and I knew what I had heard, I just didn't appreciate what I'd heard.

As I gasped from under the duvet for a bit of air I found myself saying, 'Don't do this to me, please don't do this to me.' I repeated over and over to myself the words I'd just heard 'look behind you.' Angrily I called out, 'You can get lost whoever you are.' There was no one behind me because the bed backed onto the wall. This is not funny, I wasn't amused. I felt my throat tighten as though it was being squeezed but it wasn't, it was me panicking. 'Not bloody funny at all,' I thought, wondering who was talking to me. It was the ghosts of the 'dead' who were talking to me.

I wondered if the ghosts were new, or if they had they been there all the time and I just hadn't noticed. Well, I was noticing them now. As I looked at the clock on my bedside table, it showed 1.30 am. Hubby was at work, as if I needed reminding. He had left me to deal with our uninvited house visitors, the ghosts, on my own. I looked at the clock again, it was only 1.37 am and it would be another six hours before Hubby came home. Six more long hours before the nightmare would end and I could feel safe again.

If I was to tell Mum what was happening it would frighten her, so I didn't, I was on my own with this nightmare. I didn't for one minute think I was going mad, but Mum must have thought so at times, especially one night when I accompanied her to bingo. She was pleased I wanted to go out with her which was a rare occurrence. If I didn't go out I would spend another night on my own in a house that was haunting me. How I hated sitting there like a prized pumpkin in the bingo hall. I would watch those who were lucky enough to cross off the right amount of numbers on their cards and shout, 'House'! I thought, 'Yeah right, 'house' don't remind me'!

I didn't like my house, nor did I want to be there on my own, anything could happen and it usually did. When Hubby's night shifts came round I would usually go to bed and switch on the TV for extra light. The sound of people talking on the telly made me feel better, stupid that a telly should make you feel better. If a ghost was to appear the people on the telly couldn't exactly jump out of the box and save me could they? I remember a friend once told me ghosts jumped out of her telly.... she must have been kidding! Nonetheless, the time wasn't right for me to be picturing this scene.

I snuggled up in bed with my duvet trying to concentrate on watching telly when I noticed the volume on the TV was getting louder. The adverts were on and appeared to be much louder than the programme I had previously been watching. The loudness was increasing to a level that was deafening; I had to find the remote. I fumbled under the pillow where the remote was safely tucked before I got into bed, only it wasn't there now, it was gone. I fumbled round the bed trying to find the remote to no avail. I gave up looking and decided to duck under the duvet to block out the rising noise levels. All the same, I couldn't stay under the duvet with the volume blasting out, nor did I particularly want to get up.

It was no use my hiding; that wouldn't solve the problem. Summoning up just enough courage to pop my head out from under the duvet I looked round the room. I was expecting to see something, or someone but not a soul in sight. My eyes rested on top of the telly where the remote was, 'Darn', I thought. I really needed to get up and get it as I was worried the neighbours would come round and complain. As if I didn't have enough problems, having someone come and bang on the door in the middle of the night was not something I wanted to endure.

Since the volume was unbearably deafening I decided to brave it and crawl over the bed and grab the remote. The very remote that had mysteriously ended up on top of the telly. I was fumbling with every button going in desperation to try to reduce the volume but it wouldn't budge. I felt nauseous and wanted to throw up.

I pressed the buttons trying frantically to change the channels hoping this may help but nothing happened, I had lost control of the TV. I knew the 'ghosts' were controlling it because the TV was changing from channel to channel. I was fed up and shouted out, 'Leave the telly alone.' I continued desperately pressing every button again and again with more force until finally the channel stabilised and the volume lowered. It worked, the volume decreased, the picture was fine and I switched the sound to mute.

My breathing sounded like I had been in a battle, I felt as though I had. Placing the remote under my pillow I pulled the duvet completely over me. I could just about breathe. I was fed up, utterly and totally fed up, tired and exhausted. I'd had enough and the ghosts could do what they liked, with or without my consent.

Haunted Toys

As anyone would know, waking up in the middle of the night can be annoying at the best of times. As time went on I habitually and annoyingly woke up, or was deliberately being woken up. I usually drifted off to sleep exhausted from trying to keep myself awake, it was hard work trying to stay awake. I needed to stay awake, but one night after a hard struggle trying to keep my eyes open and my mind alert in the absence of Hubby my defences collapsed. I fell off to sleep. I knew I hadn't been sleeping too long when I was woken by the sound of music. I recognised the music and had heard it often. I had left the telly on, but this music wasn't coming from the telly, it was coming from the room next door. The room next door was our spare room where Hubby kept a few Star Wars toys and Star Wars gadgets.

I lay there listening to the sound of dum dum dum dum de dum dum de dum. The music was the theme to Star Wars. I couldn't fathom out for the life of me why I should be hearing 'Star Wars' at such an ungodly hour. I reasoned with myself that Hubby had gone to work and must have set an alarm clock. Perhaps he had forgotten to turn off one of the other toys that was now playing music.

The music wouldn't stop, it sounded like a battlefield going on in there. I was really freaking out, almost to the point of passing out. I had to do something to make the noise stop. I would have to get out of bed. I lay there thinking, 'They're not my toys, they're Hubby's, he can come home and sort them out.

I reached for my mobile phone on the bedside table. Pressing the numbers to his mobile I called him, he wouldn't like it, but then neither did I. He answered asking, 'What's the matter?' I couldn't help but shout, 'Your toys are playing in the room next door.' He replied, 'They can't be, I took all the batteries out earlier in the day.' Feeling somewhat puzzled as to how I would answer this I said, 'Well something is playing on its own and I'm not amused.' He laughed. I reminded him by telling him, 'I'm here on my own with God knows who from the other side and it's not nice.' He thought he was being candidly funny when he told me to go and check what was causing the music to play. I bluntly said to him, 'I'm not going, you come home and you go in there.' adding for good measure cries of, 'this house is haunted.' He didn't laugh at that! I held the phone tightly in my hand as I relayed what had been going on in the house which he found quite amusing. He wasn't coming home much to my annoyance. I cut the call and sat there sobbing, looking around me and looking at what was going on. I tried to make sense of it all but I couldn't make sense of any of it. The music still blaring away next door gave me no choice but to get up and check it. I jumped up out of bed heading for the spare room; I was prepared to perform a quick autopsy by removing the batteries of whichever toy or 'thing' had resurrected itself.

Tired, angry and sobbing I walked across the landing to the room next door. The lights flickered on the landing and I knew something was going to happen. I took a deep breath and grabbed the door handle, kicking the door open at the same time. As I entered the room I switched on the light and then wished I hadn't! I was the centre piece to a light show similar to that in a discotheque. The light flickered rapidly. I wasn't going to turn back now and slowly made my way in looking round the room for signs of a very active toy. I was looking for something that might be waddling around, or flashing a light sabre.

I was aware that the music had suddenly stopped. I couldn't find what I was looking for; however, the room did feel eerily quiet and extremely cold. I examined all the shelves and checked the floor for movement of anything electronic or battery operated. It wasn't easy trying to find what I was looking for with the lights flickering on and off.

The room appeared to be throwing its own party with the sound of music blasting out before I entered, then the flickering of lights when I opened the door. I wasn't amused. I'm always up for a good laugh and a joke but this wasn't funny.

Standing as close to the door as I could a sudden coldness enveloped itself around me. The lights continued to flicker. I swore a few times before I made a swift exit switching off the light and slamming the door behind me. I hurried back to bed grabbing my duvet and flung it over me. I cried tears of fear. As the tears fell down my face it all went quiet, I noticed the energies in my bedroom began to change and feel calm. I cried myself to sleep.

When Hubby came home from his night shift I heard his footsteps on the stairs as he headed for the spare room. The very room where only a few hours earlier haunted toys had been holding a music and light show. He marched into our bedroom telling me it wasn't possible for any of them to have switched themselves on. Sitting up I was struggling to keep my eyes open and didn't have the strength to argue, not that we argued. Feeling like I'd had a good night out when I hadn't, I managed to drag myself out of bed to get ready for work.

I slapped on extra make-up (more art deco for the pillow) to cover my heavy bulging eyes that greeted me when I looked in the mirror. Bloody mirror, never shows what you want you to see, always what you don't want to see! I must have had quite a few birthdays in the course of a few weeks. I felt I'd aged more than I should!

I Married a Sceptic

'I'm haunted,' I kept telling myself, 'I'm haunted, the 'ghosts' are everywhere, watching me, taunting me, scaring the living daylights out of me.' I didn't dare mention half of what I heard and saw to Hubby, he was having a hard time himself, trying to explain the unexplained as it were. Things were changing, I didn't like the change, spirit was changing, and I didn't like their change either. The only person that wasn't changing was Hubby.

Many a night Hubby would pick me up from the office to take me home, but I never wanted to go home. I would have been happy to stay in the car and even happier to sleep in it, but I knew I had to get out. Standing behind Hubby I could feel myself tense as he turned the key in the door. I wished I could have walked through the door as quick as he did but I couldn't. You'd have thought I was listening and looking out for burglars as I stood on the doorstep reluctant to go in. Hubby asked if I was coming in so the door could be closed, or if I was going to stand on the step all night; I preferred the latter. We sat at the table eating dinner in quiet mode, occasionally glancing up at one another to give the odd smile.

Hubby had been trying to make conversation but I wasn't interested. I was only interested in what was happening to me, what was happening in my own house. He didn't want to talk about it. If I talked about it he would say I needed those men who come and take you away in a straight jacket. I was thankful Hubby had only one more night shift to do. Thankful I would at least soon have his company for the whole night. If anything did happen he would be the first to witness it, after me.

I would normally settle down and switch my computer on after dinner but I couldn't. I was undecided what to do for the evening so just sat in the chair and tried to read the newspapers. I couldn't even do that since all I could think about was another night on my own. But, I wouldn't be on my own would I? I begged Hubby to call in sick for the night but he wouldn't and went off to work.

I knew the spirits would keep me awake another night and could feel them already, I could hear them breathe. I muttered to myself, 'It's going to be a long night,' as I slowly walked up the stairs. I could feel a coldness that walked beside me as I reached the top of the stairs. I was fed up thinking it was just my imagination when I *knew* it wasn't.

I got in bed half dressed, and tired. I knew I had to stay awake, quite for whose sake I didn't know, but I needed to stay awake. As I lay in bed drifting in and out of sleep no longer able to keep my eyes open, part of me kept thinking, 'Ok you win, come and get me, I give up, what do you want?' Whilst another part of me kept telling them to go away and leave me alone, I'd had enough. But, they wouldn't leave me alone, the voices were still talking.

I was comfortable with my ability to hear voices and didn't mind since the voices always seemed to tell the truth. It was the seeing of ghosts and apparitions that I minded, I didn't like it, and it freaked me out. Spirit was changing the way I worked, or the way they worked, that was pretty darn obvious. They could have warned me what it was going to be like, someone could have warned me. Spirit could have told me. So, why didn't they tell me? The voices had after all been whispering to me for many years.

It was because of the voices I knew I had a different kind of ability than other 'normal' people. It was through the voices that my psychic senses developed and I began to listen more. There is no better teacher than spirit and I learnt much of what I know through their divine guidance and love. Even though spirit are the best trainers, I also recognised that spirit could have told me things change. We change, 'they' change. I used to think it was part of their plan, or my own plan that I would be tested so much. Whatever the plan, my house began to feel like an airport with ghosts and spirits flying in from all directions, but I didn't feel they liked flying out.

With Hubby at work I knew the runway would be clear for landing and my house was the control tower, but without the control. I lay in bed waiting for the arrivals until my eyes began to close. I felt myself drifting off to sleep but fighting to keep my mind and body awake. I was fighting a losing battle. My mind and body were battling one against the other, I couldn't stay awake.

My tiredness won me over; my eyelids collapsed and closed. I found myself going into a nice sleep when I was startled by a strange feeling of movement above the duvet. 'Must be me,' I told myself, 'Imagining things.' I convinced myself the duvet moved because I must have moved. 'Not a convincing theory,' I was like a stiff; I wasn't moving any inch of me.

I wasn't imagining it, the duvet was definitely moving. My head was hidden in its rightful place under the duvet and I wasn't going to peep outside. I felt something move over my arm. I felt a pressure like someone touching my arm and the feeling extended to my shoulder. 'My imagination,' I kept telling myself, 'I'm overtired and imagining things.' My heart was thumping away beating ten to the dozen when suddenly the duvet was snatched by an almighty force and thrown to the bottom of the bed.

I screamed, sat bolt upright and let out an almighty yell of, 'Get lost!' I was screaming with anger but didn't know at whom. I retrieved the duvet and snatched it back over me. Sitting up in my bed feeling angry my eyes followed a mist that started to form by the side of me.

I found myself staring at the figure of an arm, a grey transparent arm floating in mid air which disappeared gradually and slowly away from me. I sat there sobbing into the pillow, shaking with fear. I was angry that spirit dare do this. I was sobbing with fear because I couldn't understand what was going on, nor did I want to. My energy was zapped, zero, non-existent, I had no fight left in me, but fight for what, or whom?

I yelled at my spirit guide, Hannah, and told her that I wasn't at all happy. She didn't communicate anything back, or at least I didn't hear anything. I felt many spirit energies were present since the room was chillingly cold. I couldn't keep my eyes off the clock, I was hoping and praying time would pass by quickly and Hubby would be home soon.

It was 5:40am when I eventually got to sleep. Hubby shaking me broke my sleep. I'd only been asleep for two hours, if that and felt I needed more. In my state of anxiety and nervousness I relayed to Hubby the events that took place in the night. He said, 'You should see someone', further adding, 'You can't go on like this, it's making you a wreck, not to mention you can't control whatever or whoever it is haunting you. If you can't stop what's happening then you should stop working for spirit.' I thought huh, wreck, me? That was an understatement if ever I'd heard one. I knew in my heart he was right.

I couldn't understand why things were happening since all I was doing was psychic readings on the internet. I promised him I would go and seek help but that was easier said than done! I hadn't had any help so far and didn't know who to turn to. 'It's not always like this,' I said trying to reassure him. I needed that bit of reassurance for myself, let alone anyone else. I told him there must be a reason for all this to happen so suddenly.

Granted I never imagined or thought for one moment I would one day see spirit like I see them now, or as much as I see now. These spirits weren't normal, nor were some of them nice. However, I would somehow try to find help to deal with it.

I was beginning to realise spirit can be anywhere and everywhere. From my home to my workplace, they would be there, I just knew. I knew because I could sense them, I knew when I was not alone. At work, at home, I was never alone. It got so bad that after arriving home from work one time I stood on my doorstep soaking wet through the heavy downpour of rain. I should have wanted to hurry up and get indoors but I just wanted to stand on the doorstep. I rustled deep into my handbag deliberately taking time to search for my door key. I was thankful that I had so much rubbish in my bag to sift through! Retrieving the key I gently inserted it in the lock trying not to make a sound. Stupid of me; I didn't need to be quiet; if the ghosts were there they would be expecting me and could hear me anyway. My heart was racing and I could feel and taste my own fear. Fear of what to expect, fear of who would be behind the door. Panicking, I couldn't open the door, it wouldn't open. I pushed and pushed but it was stuck, this was a bad sign and that perhaps I shouldn't go in. I tried pushing the door again with an almighty shove and a few swear words until it flew open. I could see the lights flicker, a sign from spirit. 'Welcome home', I said to myself!

Hubby greeted me and we went through the usual routine, 'Hello honey, did you have a nice day?' Yeah right, nice day, my pants! I could barely stay awake all day and didn't get far searching for help on the Internet either. When I told him I searched the Internet but didn't find anything he said, 'Deal with it, give it up, come and eat your dinner.' I wasn't hungry. I sat at the table pushing the food around my plate telling him I ate earlier.

Sitting uncomfortably at the dinner table I could sense someone watching me, someone watching over me. I felt a coldness surround me yet the heating was on full. As I sat there I began to see faces in the table cloth, on the walls, the doors and the TV. I was seeing all these faces but didn't know who they were. I wasn't happy and didn't want to stay in the same room as 'them' the ghosts. I cleared the dinner table and went upstairs to the bathroom. After seeing the face in the mirror recently I was reluctant to open the door. On turning the door handle I told myself how stupid I was, it was only a bathroom, nothing in it could hurt me but I couldn't go in. Instead, I turned and stood at the door of my bedroom, hesitant to go in there as well. I didn't know what or who was behind the door, or who would be waiting for me. Someone would be waiting that much I knew.

I could feel myself shaking, getting angry and telling myself it was *my* room. I kicked the door open as if I was going in for the kill and flicked on the light. The light flickered rapidly so I switched it off then back on again, that worked, it settled itself right. There was nothing wrong with the electrics, just something wrong with the ghosts! I entered the bedroom cursing under my breath.

If Hannah, my spirit guide was with me I didn't know it. I wouldn't have been surprised if she was having a good laugh at me. However, I really didn't feel comfortable and hadn't been in the room long when I started seeing grey shapes forming on the cupboard doors. There was something just a little bit strange going on. The shapes began to form as human figures as I watched them materialise. I sat fixed on the edge of my bed not moving and not wanting to move. I sat frozen like a blob of ice watching these figures take shape.

So, there it was, on one cupboard door I saw the outline of a man, whilst on another appeared the shape of a large hand. I found myself staring at the shape of the hand consistently. The hand was not your regular sized hand; this hand was approximately three feet in height. 'Yep, that's not normal', I muttered to myself. I needed to get my bath towels out of that cupboard. As I sat pondering what to do the light suddenly flickered again and the shapes faded away until I was no longer seeing them. I turned and ran out the door and down the stairs heading for the kitchen where the lights continued to flicker. I don't mind telling you there was nothing wrong with my eye sight. I know what I saw and the lights were flickering.

I could see orbs shooting past me, moving across the ceiling and along the floor. Orbs are widely known to be that of a spiritual entity, although this has yet to be disproved. However, not wanting to explain myself if Hubby came in I pretended I was looking for something in the kitchen drawers. Spirit wasn't the only one keeping a close eye on me. I don't know who was following who, Hubby following me, me following Hubby, or spirit following me. I certainly wasn't following spirit.

I would do anything than return to my bedroom and deal with ghostly figures and apparitions. I'd captured an apparition on my camera once when I was sitting at my computer in the bedroom. I heard a female voice tell me to go and get my camera. I ignored the voice and kept on typing on the computer. The voice repeated itself, 'Get the camera.' I didn't even know why I was asked to get my camera but I did. The voice whispered, 'On the curtains, take a picture of the curtains.' I thought if spirit didn't like my curtains they could say, I wouldn't be offended!

I snapped away with the camera a few times taking pictures of the curtains, doors, walls and ceiling. I hadn't done this before, taken pictures of my room, but because of the urgency in the voice I felt I should do as I was told. When I downloaded the pictures an icy coldness enveloped me and I froze. I gazed at the computer screen and the photos I had taken. I had captured a spirit materialisation with a face in the middle of the ectoplasm, (substance produced by spiritual entities). I had taken a few photos in the same area but the manifestation only appeared in one shot. I knew why the voice, probably of my spirit guide, had asked me to get the camera.

However, I wasn't going to get my camera out now and take pictures of over sized hands or figures. I wasn't that far advanced as a psychic or anything else for that matter and it made me shiver thinking the 'dead' were with me. The memory of the photograph and the manifestation on my curtains haunted me for a long time.

I was still pretending to search for a light bulb when Hubby walked into the kitchen. I made an excuse that the bulb had blown in the bedroom. After he told me I was looking in the wrong place he grabbed a bulb from the top shelf of the cupboard. I thought he was a very brave man as he strode up the stairs. He wouldn't know what was up there! I strode up the stairs behind him, I wasn't in any hurry. I could feel myself sweating with fear and trembling as I got closer to the room. It was extremely difficult trying to act 'normal' without raising concerns.

I followed him into the room trying to smile and act normal. I couldn't see anyone or anything. I didn't know if this was good or bad. At least if there had been a ghost present Hubby could have been witness to it. Hubby changed the light bulb which didn't really need changing, or so I thought. Only now the light bulb was not working, it had blown and did need changing. Spirit had worked extremely hard with the lighting to get my attention and it was no surprise the bulb actually needed to be replaced.

I grabbed my bath towels and robe from the cupboard and headed for the bathroom. I never usually lock the door but this time I did, I wanted to keep the 'ghosts' out. Standing over the bath I ran the water and emptied a whole bottle of bubble bath into the tub without realising it. I had gone into a form of trance as I sat perched on the edge of the bath staring down into the running water. I was fixated as I stared into the shapes and faces that formed in the bubbles. It wasn't until I heard banging on the door and Hubby shouting I realised what I had done. I couldn't explain the bubbles that had risen to the brim of the bath to almost over-flowing. I opened the door and apologised to Hubby for locking it. I'm sure he thought I was suicidal. I made the excuse I'd had a hard day at work and was overly tired. It was no surprise I was tired. I left the bathroom door wide open just in case the 'ghosts' drowned me. I'd obviously been watching too many horror movies and told myself off for thinking such a stupid thing.

I sank into the bath amongst the overdose of bubbles closing my eyes, looking forward to relaxing. I couldn't relax. You know when you ask people to 'give you a minute' when you need a bit of space, well I so much wanted this 'minute.' But I wasn't going to get my minute. No sooner had I closed my eyes and rested my head on the lip of the bath I began to see strange lights zooming in front of my eyes. I opened my eyes to see a light phenomena dancing around in front of my face. I looked towards the window were there were faces on the blind. 'Stop it,' I yelled, 'Stop it, go away and leave me alone.' Not wanting to stay in the bath for fear of an 'unexplained drowning' I ran back into the bedroom.

I called down to Hubby to say I'd run his bath, anything to get him in my vicinity so the 'ghosts' would go away. I lay on the bed, hair sopping wet, no enthusiasm at all to dry it with the dryer. How I hated wet hair. I had to dry it, so I grabbed the dryer and switched it on brushing the water out of my hair. All was going well until the dryer suddenly stopped. I flicked the switch to the 'on' position but nothing happened. After a few more unsuccessful attempts it was clear it wasn't going to work so I threw it on the floor in anger.

I was irritated I had to live this way. I wanted to put the TV on but decided against it, there was no point since 'ghosts' would be featuring in their own programme. I told Hubby we should have an early night and watch TV in bed. I had no intention of sleeping, or anything else for that matter. He agreed to my request, anything to keep me happy and came to bed.

Noticing my hair was wet Hubby asked why I hadn't bothered to dry it. I duly explained the dryer was broken. Picking it up he switched it on and found nothing to be wrong with it, it was working perfectly fine. I had to listen to hubby as he said, 'Nothing wrong with that.' I replied, 'It didn't work for me because it kept cutting out.' Bloody 'ghosts' at it again I thought. He switched the TV on and I took a quick glance to see if I could see anything, although why I wanted to see anything was bizarre because there was nothing I wanted to 'see.' I certainly didn't want to see the 'ghosts.

The TV looked ok. I didn't want to watch it though because I knew what was going to happen. Instead I laid back and closed my eyes for a while. I hadn't closed them for long when I was seeing faces flashing past my eyes. 'For heaven's sake,' I muttered angrily. It wasn't long either before I heard Hubby snoring, how bloody annoying! It concerned me because if he was snoring - who was looking out for the 'ghosts! I nudged him and told him to shut up, it took quite a few more hard nudges before he fully woke up and got back to showing an interest in the TV again. This made me feel better but it didn't do much for him!

I glanced at the TV and saw another face in the corner of the screen, it wasn't changing, yet the scenes on the programme were. I whispered to Hubby, 'Do you see a face in the corner of the screen?' He answered, 'No', then I told him to focus and he said, 'Yes', he did see it and how weird it was. Hang on here, rewind please, hey he saw it! He couldn't explain it nor did he want to. I knew now it wasn't my imagination, nor was it Hubby's, and he certainly wasn't agreeing with me just to shut me up, or for peace and quiet.

I am sane, honest, I'm not going crazy, delusive or anything else, I really was seeing 'ghosts' Great! I could now see but I was having other problems in hearing, there wasn't any voices speaking to me now, what was going on? Where was my spirit guide, Hannah? Why was she not sorting these spirits out? What use was a spirit guide if they didn't do anything you told them to?

When finally Hubby had had enough of watching the telly he switched it off turning the lights off too. It would be darkness once again, am I bothered? (See me smile here). I hadn't moved the stool by the side of my bed which I had used to sit on whilst drying my hair. I was now worried that I may fall over it during the night should I need to get out of bed that is. Fat chance of that, I was staying fixed to the sheets tonight. Tonight I was going to sleep like a baby. Yeah right, of course I would!

And so it goes, one minute I'm sleeping like the baby I had envisaged, or perhaps more like the mature calm woman I am supposed to be, the next minute I was opening my eyes to see an Indian man kneeling by my bedside. He was wearing a turban and looked like someone from 'Aladdin and the Forty Thieves' if you get the picture. His torso above his waistline was naked, except for a medallion on a chain. His eyes were big and brown, his lashes long. How do I know this? He was staring me right in the face!

He was pulling on the duvet and mumbling something. I couldn't hear what he was saying and I couldn't lip read either, but he seemed to be panicking over something. Well, he could panic all he liked; I shot under the duvet and nudged Hubby awake. I was asking stupidly, 'Did you see that man?' He was not amused nor did he see what I saw.

Hubby nodded off again to la-la land and a deep sleep where zzzzz's were once again quite audible. Nothing wrong with my ears apparently they were working just fine, too fine for my liking. I lay there for a while trying my best to see this man but he never came back, fed up waiting I pulled the duvet over leaving just my eyes peering out above it.

It wasn't long before I felt someone breathing in my face, cold wisps of air. I woke up to the turban man once again dancing in front of my face on top of the duvet. This time he was just two feet tall and looked like a Punch and Judy puppet, that's the size he was. I was angry and told him to, 'Get lost, go away and leave me alone.' He was hard work but he went.

After he went it suddenly dawned on me perhaps he couldn't speak English let alone understand it. I was beside myself. I couldn't wake Hubby up for fear of getting a telling off so I lay there, eyes wide open, same old scenario. I rolled over and faced Hubby thinking the view from his side may prove more 'normal' and fell back to sleep.

The alarm went off at 3.45am, time for Hubby to get up and venture off to work, it was still dark. I was still scared. I could hear the rain bashing against the windows and the coldness of the night around me. As Hubby left the room I could feel someone watching me, someone standing very close watching over me. I got up and turned the main light on; I didn't want to stay in the dark, stay alone by myself in the dark room.

I heard the front door close as Hubby left the house. The main light in my room flickered as I counted, once, twice, three times, four times and it didn't stop. Angrily I shouted out, 'Stop it, enough!' Whoever was playing with the light switch stopped. I reached over and touched the light on my bedside table then inched my way over the bed to the wall and turned the main light off. I found myself saying, 'Thank you,' when the light stopped flickering. Imagine that, me saying, 'Thank you.' but to whom?

Someone was paying attention when I said, 'Stop.' I was very much relieved. I was relieved but still nervous to the point of exceedingly frightened. Here I was all alone in my house, (not quite alone, Mum was sleeping next door) with visitors from the other side, no big deal, or so it seemed. Exhausted I fell off to sleep.

I didn't have to get up for work the next day; instead I spent the day keeping busy by venturing out down the town. I treated myself to some therapeutic shopping by purchasing dull looking black clothes. It helped take my mind off the ghosts. At least when I did go home I had something new for them to look at. I wasn't sure who I was buying my new frocks for, me or 'them'!

By the time I got home, I found I was thinking the same old thing again as I stood on the doorstep wondering who would be waiting for me. I even wondered if any of my furniture or objects had moved out of place. I needed not fear since all was well as I entered the hallway breathing a sigh of relief. I couldn't gather up enough courage to go upstairs to hang my nice new clothes on hangers, I left them in the bag.

I wanted to put the telly on but was too afraid; if the truth be known I was too afraid to move from one room to another. Silly feeling but it's the truth. The rest of the day passed by quite slowly, I was at a loss as what to do. I remembered the books I had bought off the Internet and took them off the shelf. I would read anything to distract my thoughts, except go on the computer.

I had been reading as a clairaudient (psychic ability to hear clearly) for almost two years, I was still new in listening to the different types of voices I found myself hearing. I knew I had no need to doubt the voices since the information they gave was always truthful. I loved giving readings over the Internet to people who visited the chat room I visited. I used to sit there night after night typing messages from their loved ones in spirit. I was giving validation that the voice I was hearing and the messages I was transmitting were from the person they knew to be deceased.

Whilst it makes me happy to give messages to others it also saddens me because it seems unfair that the person receiving the message cannot see or hear the deceased spirit. I know how much they long to see and hear them. I know many people here on the earth plane would love an opportunity to be able to talk to the deceased, even if it was just the once.

Because I spent a great deal of time on the Internet giving messages to people it helped to strengthen my psychic communications with the spirit world. I'd only have to read a few words and I would hear a spirit talking to me. Sometimes I would see a spirit in my mind that would come and stand by my side. As my messages were getting stronger, my spiritual side grew. I hadn't realised by how much, I hadn't realised just how much I was evolving as a spiritual messenger. I also hadn't realised how much I had been attracting spirit into my home.

It wasn't just voices I would hear, I would also see black and white or coloured images of people I had never met. These images were projected through my mind as soon as my head hit the pillow. It was strange how these images would flash past in the matter of a split second. Some were nice, some not so nice.

When the weekends came I found I couldn't summon up the courage to do the clothes washing. All I had to do was put the clothes in the machine. Not so hard but it meant moving from room to room around the house. If I was downstairs I would have to go upstairs and get the washing. The washing stayed in the basket until Hubby came home. I would busy myself with the housework downstairs first.

The radio would be switched on to a music channel as I did the hovering, dusting and polishing. The radio would change channels; I'd change channels back again and issue the odd command of, 'Stop it.' The bottom part of the house looked and felt exceptionally clean, to my Hubby's delight I hasten to add. He must have thought he had got his 'old' wife back!

Once Hubby was home I would go upstairs, get the washing, bring it down and stick it in the machine, making sure it would get dried and ironed the same evening. By 9 o'clock I would usually be tired but didn't want to go to bed, well not on my own. I would often talk Hubby into an early night watching TV upstairs. He would be quite pleased to do whatever it took to make me rest.

As soon as I got in bed I could see a figure walk past the bottom of my bed. It was another one of those grey transparent figures (ghost) that looked like a wisp of mist floating by. I lay there bravely watching it as it passed through the wall but it was gone in a matter of seconds. I felt nervous, nervous that this figure would return. I fell off to sleep with Hubby still watching TV. It was 1.30am when I awoke to find him switching off the telly and the lights. I made sure I had one last visit to the bathroom before I settled down. I didn't want to get up in the middle of the night.

As soon as the lights went out and Hubby was tucked up in bed beside me I saw a dark figure standing by my bed. I yelled, 'Get lost.' The figure went and I continued with my sleep. It wasn't long before I woke up to find a man sitting on the stool by my bed, the very stool I should have put back in the corner of the room a few nights ago. I rubbed my eyes and opened them wide to make sure I wasn't dreaming. I wanted to make sure I wasn't seeing or imagining things, and nope I wasn't, this man was for real. He was sitting there large as life wearing a wide brimmed straw hat, red and white pinstriped cut off trousers and a white short sleeved shirt.

I didn't like what I saw, so I moved over the other side of the bed to where my husband was and frantically poked him in the back causing him to almost fall out of bed. 'Did you see him, did you see him?' I yelled. Looking back over my shoulder I saw the man dissolve into thin air as I was screaming out. Hubby shouted 'What the heck is going on, (not quite the words he used) there's no one there, get back to sleep,' he said with a sigh of annoyance. 'There was a man sitting on the stool,' I yelled, now feeling stupid for thinking he would wake up and see what I saw.

I was mesmerised by this man, who was he? Why was he here? Why did he come to me? Why didn't he stay so Hubby could see him? How did he disappear the way he did? Why did he sit there looking at me? I wanted to see this man again, I wanted him to come back, I found myself willing him to come back. I waited for what seemed like hours but in fact it was only an hour. There was still no sign of the man, he wasn't coming back. I lay there stupidly thinking that if I had ghosts then perhaps my neighbours had them too. It was just a thought, probably a stupid one at the time.

I went back to sleep without any further disturbances. Trying to reason with Hubby the next morning about my visitation from the other side was almost impossible. Whilst he didn't disbelieve me he didn't believe me either, nor did I expect him to, why should he? I must admit I was beginning to feel a little relaxed about seeing 'ghosts', but I was still nervous at the same time. I felt relaxed because I wasn't hurt or harmed in any way. Some days were good, some were bad. Being honest, they were mostly bad as I had got into a routine of being woken up in the middle of the night by spiritual strangers. I got into a routine of feeling totally knackered before doing a full day's work at the office.

After work I would spend hours on the phone talking to friends. I couldn't talk to my family as they didn't believe in ghosts and thought it all to be a load of poppycock to put it mildly. Everyone is entitled to their own belief system, why should my family believe something just because I do. I was to find out over time that some of my family members were in fact psychic themselves. This didn't surprise me, often I would bring home the same cake, biscuits or chocolates as Mum had bought earlier in the day.

My aunt told me she believed my grandmother had been psychic. I used to think my Nan knew things about people too. My niece in Australia told me she was seeing things but didn't reveal this until she emigrated. My other niece sees ghostly apparitions in her house and place of work. My niece's daughters both see and feel spirit.

My older brother, who has always been a sceptic and not keen on the paranormal, had witnessed the ghost of my sister's fiancé walking towards him. My brother had been working in a street some distance from where we lived at the time. He had never told me this until two years ago. He had kept it to himself for all those years. He also kept to himself the materialisation of my mother soon after she had passed away. He had seen her sitting in the same chair she had always sat in. Psychics have run in our family apparently for a number of years, only some wouldn't admit to being psychic. I never wanted to admit I was psychic; it was other people telling me I was.

I was gradually getting used to it all, but I was totally fed up, very tired and found myself going along with the flow and the moment. It didn't concern me when I was downstairs and saw someone pass behind me, or saw movement out of the corner of my eye. It didn't bother me if the lights flickered either because I only had to say, 'Stop,' and it would stop.

I was still bothered by the changing energies around me, when I kept going cold for no apparent reason. I would feel cold around my face, hands or my feet and feel a tingling in my hair, or someone brush over my head with a soft gentleness. One day I laughed when Hubby said he had crashed out on the bed and woke up to the sensation of someone stroking his hair. He was on his own at the time. This proved it wasn't my imagination as I knew my Hubby to be a rational type of guy. He remained sceptic.

Apparitions

I thought I had got to know the ways of spirit quite well, when in reality I hadn't. I learnt something new every day. Many days were challenging, but I had yet to face my biggest spiritual challenge.

I got used to feeling the presence of energies (spirit) around me, energies that constantly changed and could make me feel cold. What I hadn't been used to was how forceful spirit energy could be. Everyday would be different in the types of energy I would feel, often I knew if the energy was good or bad by the heaviness that surrounded me.

There was an energy I felt to be so forceful one night that I began to feel more than a little concerned. I was aware of its presence around me most of the day. I was also aware it had attached itself to me. It was so strong that I thought I kept seeing it walk past me. I thought my mind was playing tricks on me as I couldn't be sure if I was seeing someone, or if it was my imagination. I had never doubted anything I had seen in the past but this was different.

It was because this energy disturbed me that I made a point of going to bed the same time as Hubby. I was beginning to wonder who was the most nervous around the house, me or Hubby. Although I was feeling a little uneasy with the heavy energy I was experiencing I decided not to take any notice. I drifted off to sleep. I hadn't been sleeping long when I woke up and glanced at the clock, it was 3.30am. My eyes moved away from the clock to the wardrobe where I was met with a glowing green apparition of a man's face. I looked at the face thinking, 'This can't be real.' I rubbed my eyes for good measure but the face was still there. It wasn't a dream.

As I gazed at the apparition I noticed a remarkable resemblance to Hubby's facial features. This man was talking to me, his mouth was moving but I couldn't hear any sound. I was shaking with fear as this was something else new to me, a bloody glow in the dark face talking to me. I didn't even bother waking Hubby up as I knew he would be annoyed; instead I turned over to face in the opposite direction and stared at the wardrobe there. I didn't want to close my eyes and was glad I didn't, the man's face had appeared on that wardrobe too. He was there again talking to me, his lips moving but still no voice.

I looked at him as he was speaking and mouthed back at him, 'Get lost.' I felt anger well up inside me, anger that came with fear. I didn't know what to do as there was nothing that I could do. I couldn't exactly get out of bed, grab him by the throat and march him out of my house. He wasn't physical and he wasn't from this dimension, I was in serious need of talking to someone.

It was no use; I had to take a day off work. I phoned in and booked myself a day's holiday. I couldn't sit at home all day so decided to nip round to see one of my friends and talk to her about the events of the night before. She didn't know what to make of it but it was soon going to be made very obvious. As I was chatting away to her my mobile phone rang, it was Hubby calling from work, his voice was clearly distressed. I could hardly hear him as he sounded upset. I had never heard him this way before and wondered what on earth was wrong. After some hesitation from his end he informed me his mother had passed away during the night with a heart attack. It was a sudden shock for us all, she hadn't been ill so it was a shock that she had passed over. He was on his way to pick me up.

I remembered that the glowing face of the man on my wardrobe the night before had looked familiar. I was almost sure his facial features resembled those similar to Hubby's family, yet, I couldn't understand what I was looking at, who, or why. What I didn't know at the time was that the man was a messenger from spirit. I began to feel guilty; I began to feel I could have helped her, if only I'd known. I had received the message but couldn't interpret it.

We were only talking about going to visit my mother-in law the following weekend, it was too late now. It didn't make any sense that she had passed away especially as it was my dad who was terminally ill. My dad had been suffering for a short period with lung cancer and not expected to live in his physical body much longer.

It was all too much for me to take in. I was exhausted, drained and confused by what was happening. I was even more confused my spirit guide wasn't talking to me, or was she? I was fed up with my house being taken over by non physical beings. I had ghosts of the 'dead' living with me. I had to get help.

I tried to get help from a Spiritual church, but they were reluctant to help me and gave no advice whatsoever. In fact, I remember the lady at the church stood with her back to me tending to flowers and not bothering to turn round to face me. I was trying to explain some of the things that were going on. I begged for help but was more or less told it was my own fault because I used a computer. I was left to my own devices once again and became a spiritual kind of warrior, going through one battle after another with ghosts, spirits and the living.

Taking the advice given to me by the lady at the church I did stop working on my computer but it didn't help; it didn't solve the problem and spirit was still there haunting me. My own thoughts began to haunt me knowing my dad's physical life was limited. The night before he passed to the spirit world I had lain in bed thinking of him. I was thinking how much he must be suffering. As I was thinking of Dad my eyes were drawn to the chest of drawers almost opposite me. I found myself staring at lots of signatures appearing one by one, the signatures covered all the six drawers. There were hundreds and hundreds being written as I laid there gazing in admiration. And, as if the signatures weren't magical enough, a bouquet of flowers appeared floating in the air with a long red ribbon and a card placed strategically between the flowers. I felt a sense of peace fill the room but didn't feel frightened; nonetheless, I wasn't getting up to see what was written on the card!

The next morning I got a call to tell me my father had passed away but I already knew. Losing someone before Christmas is hard but to lose two people was even harder. I don't believe in coincidences but the funerals of my mother in law and my father were to be held on the same day at the same time ... in different crematoriums.

My husband went to his mother's funeral and I went to my father's funeral. Words cannot express how I felt, how we felt. You think it couldn't happen to you and that this sort of thing only happens to other people. Anything can happen at any time to anyone.

In the early hours of the day of my dad's funeral I was awakened at 4.40am with the sound of music and a choir singing. I perched my head up off the pillow to listen to where it was coming from. My first annoying thought was that it must be coming from the neighbours next door. As I listened more intently I realised how beautiful the music was and how beautiful the voices were. I began to realise it was the music and voices of the Angels singing and a sign that Dad had been welcomed into the spirit world. It was the most beautiful music and glorious choir I had ever heard. The Angels sang for both my dad and mother-in-law.

Later in the day of dad's funeral a friend was to stay at his house till we returned. She was organising the food, teas and coffees. When we returned I noticed how her face looked pale and ashen, as though she had seen a ghost. She was shaking as she told me the toilet kept flushing. I didn't know this lady and she didn't know me. I was happy as Larry though as I knew this was Dad's way of saying he was still here. Quite why he used the toilet to indicate his presence I will never know. To my knowledge, the toilet has been in good working order ever since.

I still had my problem though and it wasn't going away. I was still upset, angry and fed up with spirit. I had been going through hell in my own home. I was always creeping around in the hope that I wouldn't disturb any ghost, or worse still attract their attention. Stupid thing to do I know.

I was living a nightmare and going to bed was getting increasingly difficult. I hated going to bed and being taunted by the 'dead.' However, I felt excited and somewhat honoured that I had had a choir of Angels sing to me the night before. I was sure getting to sleep would not be such a problem anymore.

I obviously wasn't psychic enough to see what was in store the night after Dad's funeral. I had managed to fall off to sleep without any problem but then woke up for no reason. Yet, there was a reason as I noticed the figure of a man at the bottom of my bed. The man was wearing a lovely blue knitted jumper with a shirt underneath. I couldn't see his face because his head wouldn't keep still as it twisted whilst spinning round on his shoulders. I sat there gazing at him for a few seconds before telling him to, 'Get lost.' To my surprise that worked, that felt good, he went!

Settling back to sleep it wasn't long before I woke up again, my gaze fixed to the corner of my room where my chair was situated. I was intrigued as I found myself looking at three small children, two boys and a girl, all with their hands above their brows searching for something or someone. I was more annoyed that they had used my chair to stand on and shouted to them, 'Get off my chair!' Adding for good measure, 'You wouldn't do that in your own home.' Imagine that, brave little me saying that! The children faded away into the night just as the man had done, what a heck of a night it was, yet it was not over. There was more!

There was to be a third visit from spirit, this time I was woken up by an elderly gentleman perched on my stool beside my bed. The man was smoking a pipe and looking at me. I was tired and irritated so told him to, 'Get lost.' I wanted to be left alone and found myself begging him to go away. I'd had enough.

Haunted by Ghosts

Ghosts we associate with 'dead' people, right? Since I had got mildly used to Hannah speaking to me I couldn't ignore what she told me. Her view on 'dead' people helped to change my view. It also helped to put me at ease when she told me, 'You can't tell spirit people to go away because you are telling someone's Mother, Father, Grandfather, Grandmother, Son, Daughter, Husband or Wife to go. You are telling all these spirits who have gathered energy and found you to go away'. It is your duty to help them cross over into the light. Hannah told me to be more 'respectful' and 'do not fear'.

I thought about what Hannah had said and knew she was right, I was being rude to the 'dead' people. It made me change my way of thinking about the 'afterlife' and the 'people' in the 'afterlife.' I decided the only way I could change and face my fear was to face my fear … the 'dead.' I decided *I* was going to be in control and not spirit. It was *my* house and *my* home, not theirs!

Full of anger and rage I marched up the stairs and stormed into my bedroom, cursing under my breath. If I was going to end my nightmare, now would be the right time to do it. I was just in the mood for it. I was going to give them the same hell as they gave me. I jumped with great force onto my bed hoping that they were the ones who could feel *my* energy and not me theirs. I was angry. As I sat on the bed with my legs crossed I looked round the room resenting spirit. I resented how I had been treated over the last few months and how I had lived in my own home. I had gone through so much and done so much it just didn't seem fair. I wanted my life back and I was now going to change everything so I could be 'ME' again. Spirit was going to listen to 'ME', I had a lot to say and they were going to listen and like it or sod off!

I wasn't giving up this battle and I was set to give it all I had with not an ounce of fear inside me. Sitting on the bed I knew exactly what I needed to do. Making no bones about it I firmly told spirit to, 'Get out of my house and home.' I said it as though I meant it, I did mean it and I did want them to go. I told everyone from spirit to leave, except my family. I told any spirit in my house they weren't welcome or invited. I would be the one in total control of what goes on in my home. I told my spirit guide, Hannah, and any other guides, if there were any with me, to leave as I felt they were no use to me. I only wanted spirit guides who could teach me wisdom, bring me knowledge and strengthen my psychic energies and abilities. Most of all I wanted a guide who would listen to me.

As I was reciting this anger and this closure I felt the atmosphere and energies around me lift. I felt the coldness that had surrounded me drift away and felt a huge sense of relief and satisfaction. I can honestly say I thoroughly enjoyed the moment. I felt as though I'd got my home back, my life back, but most of all I found courage within to confront my fears. As I let go of the fear all the anger subsided and I found myself smiling, something I hadn't done in as many months.

The nights and weeks that followed would bring peace and harmony to my home, I felt at peace. I stopped seeing faces everywhere I looked and began to feel more comfortable and relaxed, something I hadn't done for a long time. If anything happened with my electrics I would ask spirit to stop and it would. I was in control, me myself and I. I was communicating with spirit on another level, my level. I was getting used to spirit visitations in the middle of the night.

The visitations didn't stop; I would wake up to see a ghostly figure standing by my bed, or at the bottom of my bed. Instead of telling whoever it was to go, I would ask the spirit to step into it the white light (a tunnel of pure white light that can suddenly appear as a connection to the spirit world for the deceased to travel through). It felt good I could do this, and when visited by one lady standing by my bedside smiling I was able to tell her to go into the light. The lady looked at me smiling and waving as she stepped into the white light. I smiled back at her saying, 'You will be ok now - you can go home'.

Whenever I could I would spend time looking at ways to go forward with what I had learned. If it wasn't for Hannah, my spirit guide putting it in a gentle way about spirit, who they belonged to, and that they were someone's family I believe I may not have spiritually progressed. I believe I may still be swearing and shouting at them all.

My bedtimes were now a much calmer affair. My state of mind ready for any unwelcome intruders, ready for anyone who would dare interrupt my sleep. I was ready when I woke up to see a pair of mans legs wearing blue trousers by my bed. That was all I saw, a pair of mans legs. Looking at the image stood before me I said 'You need to do better than that if you want my attention, luvvie; I'm not talking to a pair of pants that's for sure.

Within seconds more of the body started to appear, the upper body with folded arms materialised followed by the head. The materialisation was an Indian man wearing a turban. He looked down at me and moved his head in a huff and a tut, the kind of way some people do when they believe someone isn't good enough. His energy dispersed until he was no longer visible. 'Wow,' I thought, 'I did it, I did it, I did it! Yes! Yes! Yes!' I'd faced my fear and spoke out loud and had been heard, 'Yippee!

I was feeling good and when going to bed I was prepared for the 'expected.' So, when one night when Hubby came to bed later than me I was in fits of giggles. He had turned the bedside lamp off (the one with a mind of its own), but when he got into bed the lamp came on (smile). He got out of bed walked round to my side and switched it off. He got back into bed and the lamp came on again. I waited until this had happened three times before I told spirit to pack it in.

Feeling restless I put one of my earplugs in and listened to the radio hidden under my pillow. It was strange because I felt a need to open my eyes, I often felt this when spirit was present. When they were present, instead of prodding me I'd hear them talking to me, telling me to open my eyes. As I opened my eyes I noticed Hubby sit bolt upright for a few seconds before getting out of bed. I thought it was strange in the way he sat bolt upright instead of turning to get out of bed. I thought it strange too that he had a golden glow about him.

I removed the ear plug placing it under the pillow whilst patiently waiting for him to return from the bathroom. I thought this was where he had gone. I patted his pillow and nearly had a flipping heart attack as I felt his head and body lying next to mine. I wasn't dreaming, I know what I saw. I didn't close my eyes but waited for something else to happen. Quite what I was waiting for I hadn't got a clue.

I waited and waited looking out into the dark room when I noticed Hubby take the same position as before, sitting bolt upright, but this time he just laid back into his body. Wow, this was something else! I stared, trying not to blink and was glad I didn't because floating about his head was another head, not mine but that of a woman in her seventies. The materialisation of the head was grey in colour with curly hair. I didn't know this woman so I poked her in the face telling her not to take my husband out at night without asking me first. The head dispersed and disappeared. The next morning I asked Hubby who the woman was he had taken out the night before. He couldn't remember anything about it, or that he had had any dream. I smiled.

Not to be outdone by strange phenomena or weird visitations from spirit I began to look forward to my nightly visits, believe it or not. Going to bed became the highlight of my day. The experiences I had also contributed to my research in the paranormal. Everything that was happening to me was for a reason, a reason I could use perhaps to write this book. A book I started almost six years ago but never finished until now. I know I had not had enough experience, or understood enough to be able to finish it until recently.

Visitations from the 'dead' became a regular occurrence. There was a night I awoke to see my mum sitting at the bottom of my bed with her back facing me, she was shaking her head. There was nothing to sit on at the bottom of my bed so this observation puzzled me. I went to call out, 'Are you alright Mum?' when I saw the figure of a man appear and stand next to her. The figure was glowing in a bright white light, the kind of light you would most probably see your spirit guide in. The man was wearing a white shirt with black stitching round the collar and cuffs. Gazing at his head, just to make sure there was one, I noticed he was also wearing a Stetson. He was talking to Mum which was the reason why I believe she was shaking her head. I couldn't hear what he was saying so I can only assume it was something to do with me and my mum. I grew to like going to bed and seeing ghosts, I didn't mind being haunted any more.

Haunted Voices

The voices had always been there. I began to know what was going to happen in people's lives, sometimes in my own life too. I would know about things before they happened, not everything, but just things. Why it was only particular things I was to know about I cannot explain. I couldn't pick and choose what things I or anyone else needed information about. The information would come through a voice communication from spirit if there was one to give. Sometimes I would get information or answers to questions without asking, it was strange.

Following my sister's death and my curiosity about an explanation of the voices, I needed to find out more. I ventured out to a Psychic Fayre to get a reading from either a medium or a tarot reader. I choose the medium. I sat in front of her not knowing what to expect. I now know this is how my clients' react when sat in front of me, what should they expect? More to the point I now say the same when a client is with me. I never know what to expect either, the system works both ways.

Sitting nervously in front of the medium my sister came through with a message. Goose bumps formed on my arms and the hair on the back of my neck stood up. I went all cold as the medium gave me my sister's name. I wasn't sure if I wanted to hear from my sister, well I was sure, yes I did want to hear from her but I found it a little upsetting and tears welled up in my eyes.

I sat listening nervously to the medium giving me evidence of my sister's survival. She was relaying things about me, about my family, and about my sister that she couldn't possibly know. I grabbed a tissue out of my bag to wipe my eyes from the tears that had been running down my face.

By the end of the sitting I was smiling and not upset at all. I felt a big sense of relief that my sister was alive and well, she was happy, she had noticed things and she had given me guidance from beyond the grave. One of her instructions was not to delve into the paranormal until I had done as she asked in the message. Her message to me at the time was that I wasn't ready. I promised her I wouldn't do anything until I had done more research and done more training. It was only later I found out what she meant, especially about the research. I also found how she would protect me whilst she was on the other side.

I re-visited the same medium a year later, she didn't remember me, after all why should she, she sees lots of people. I received another message from my sister, this time she told me how proud she was that I had done the research, read the books, completed courses, practiced endlessly and kept my faith in spirit. I was 'dead chuffed'! She said I was ready to work as a channel for spirit.

I also visited a tarot reader at another Psychic Fayre. The tarot reader told me to go and buy my own tarot cards so I could find the answers. I looked at her and thought how rude she was, if not, a little sarcastic. A few days later I bought my own cards, contrary to superstition, if you buy your own cards you will receive bad luck. I'm not a very superstitious person so it didn't bother me.

Looking back at how the reading went and what the tarot reader told me, I knew why I was to buy my own deck of cards. I learnt the tarot and took a couple of courses with a college. I received in return for all my hard work three diplomas thank you very much! The courses included a diploma in Clairvoyance too. When I think about the diplomas I wonder why I worked so hard to get them. I mean who were they for, me or other people? Did it matter to others that I gained diplomas? It certainly didn't make any difference to my work, no one asked for any qualifications. I was a little disappointed in this but I reassured myself in knowing that I could do what I trained to do. Just as a hairdresser, beautician, builder etc invest and train in their skills, so I invested and trained in mine.

The cards gave me inspiration and a deeper understanding of events that occur in people's lives. I also know that through my training and using the cards I was to open my clairaudience (psychic clear seeing) channel wider. Spirit would come in and expand through voice or vision on what the card was revealing. I didn't really need the cards as spirit would mostly do their own job of interpreting them. Nonetheless, I love working with tarot and could use both the tarot as a divination tool and the voice of spirit to help with my psychic work.

Spirit voices would not limit themselves to helping me read tarot, or whisper to me when I worked on my computer giving readings, they would also try to talk to me through my radio. I'd only have to turn my radio on when I was in bed at night and hear a voice talking over the presenter. The voices I heard would be slurred, sometimes talking quickly, sometimes long and drawn out. Sometimes I would hear my name spoken. I'd shudder and turn the radio off.

I missed the talk show at nights, so after a while I plucked up courage, dumped the fear factor and continued to listen to my radio. I know there are times when a radio station may have interference, but I also knew that I wasn't listening to interference. It appeared spirit would find various ways of communicating with me. It was always an experience.

Haunted Workplace

There were many times during spirit's trial runs of working with me that I didn't feel comfortable. There were countless times when it wasn't easy going to work feeling like I did ... knackered, which didn't make me feel like being very sociable. My experiences of working with spirit had been sporadic and not always consistent. Many things I had been learning had been difficult to understand, let alone explain. Sometimes I couldn't understand or explain how I worked with them, or how they with me.

Soon after my Dad's passing, and after being out of work for quite a few months I was able to temp at a higher learning institute. I was excited but nervous. I was nervous because spirit had chosen the wrong time to change the way they worked with me. I had never seen or heard so many spirits and ghosts in my life, I wasn't happy.

I was battling my way through many late nights, getting up for work on time was proving to be a nightmare. I hated being late for work. However, there were times when I was late and would have to make up the time during my lunch hour. I would sit at my desk eyes stinging from lack of sleep; my mind would be all over the place. Ghosts were waking me up in the middle of the night, I couldn't sleep.

I had seen many ghosts since my Dad passed away and I wasn't quite used to it. I had also seen many spirits, mostly in my mind. I couldn't talk to anyone in my new job about my problem with these 'visitors' because it was my battle, '*One woman's battle amongst ghosts, spirits and the living.*' If the truth was known, I was too embarrassed to talk about it.

Being new to my workplace and colleagues I couldn't exactly sit down over a cup of tea and talk about the 'dead' with them. Well, not at first anyway because I didn't really know them. Because of my belief system and my ability to speak to the 'dead', it was hard for me to make friends. I found some people were a bit cautious of me, perhaps a little afraid of me. Some thought I had nothing better to do than to read their minds, the very thought made them feel a little uncomfortable. It made me feel uncomfortable knowing what they were thinking I wasn't thinking. As it happened, I had better things to do than read minds.

Nonetheless, I would have accepted any invitation to enjoy lunch with my colleagues sometimes, but never got an invite. I didn't fit in, well; at least that's what I thought. I hardly ever talked about what I did since my belief system was not the same as everyone shared. That's not to say some people had begun to think different after a psychic reading with me.

However, I think I got a little paranoid one day. I had almost caught up on my work load and ready to go home. I just had one more letter to type and I would be finished. As I typed the letter on my computer I saw words appear on the screen that made me jump back in my chair. The words on the screen read, *'This is us and we are here!'* I looked at the screen again in case I was suffering from impaired vision but the words were still there, *'This is us and we are here'*.

I knew I had seen those words before at another company I had worked at, but was uncertain as to what they meant. Perhaps I did know what 'they' meant. I couldn't understand this message the first time I had seen it, let alone seeing it twice. If anyone had come into my office I could perhaps explain my paranoia, the paranormal I could not explain. I didn't bother to save the letter; instead I hurriedly closed the computer down and ran out the door. My office was 'haunted.' Whoever 'us' were could stay there!

I'd worked in quite a few offices over the years, yet I was never surprised when spirit gave me a helping hand. If 'they' were there they were certainly helping with my tasks. Sometimes I felt like I had a built in trigger button that could access information without me realising. An example of this on/off button was when I had thought during the course of the night about a 'new' idea I could implement at the office. I didn't quite know why I was typing it up, in my own time, but I knew I could produce it to my manager the next day. He would be pleased. When he phoned to tell me of his 'new' idea I was rather excited, his idea was the same as mine! I tried to explain to him that I had already done the work, he wasn't listening. I tried again to explain it was done already. I gave up trying.

Whilst the office's I worked in may appear to have been 'haunted' I got used to it. It was a case of having to. I actually thought my kettle was haunted too when I would arrive in the mornings to find it hot. Knowing no one else could be in the office I became puzzled as to why the kettle would be hot. This went on for weeks, despite asking other people outside my office if they had been using the appliance, no one would own up. It wasn't till I left a note for the cleaner asking if she was using it I got my answer. The kettle never got hot again!

What was spooky though was when I was asked to type up a schedule for a forth coming seminar. It was easy enough, I had typed many before, except this schedule was different, it had a mind of its own. I heard a voice telling me to change one of the timings on the schedule. No matter how many times I tried to type in the correct information I kept making a mistake. The voice was nagging me until I made the change, I was right to do so. The timing had changed and the person who wrote the schedule was quite surprised I had made the change. He was surprised the change was for the correct time slot! The evidence spoke for itself, I predicted a future change. Well, not me actually, the thanks went to spirit.

The longer I worked at the Institute the more I liked it. I worked amongst academics that I could learn from. They could offer me logical theories and explanations of the mind and the paranormal, or at least try. In turn I would often offer an alternative theory and explanation of my own. The more I learned the more knowledge I gained. I began to think more rationally about psychic energy. Thinking rationally influenced my determination to do my own psychic investigative research. I still had a battle working alongside those who feared the very thing I believed in, the 'dead'.

As things settled down with the ghosts so did my mind. I began to find I was able to control spirits and ghosts better. I was able to demonstrate my psychic ability on a higher and more professional level. That wasn't to say at first I used to think any request I had for a psychic or tarot reading was made with the intention of having a good laugh at my expense. However, spirit never let me down when it came to the deceased communicating with me. I would thank God there was spirits who would communicate with me.

People would be pleased to receive messages from their loved ones; it gave them comfort knowing their loved ones were so close to them. For me, I felt happy their loved one could make that link. Of course, I would congratulate spirit and thank them for being exceptionally good at what they themselves were able to do. I couldn't do what I do without their help.

I got to know quite a lot about my work colleagues through their request for readings. I would often tell them things of significance. I would often predict what they could expect to happen at future dates. They often came back and confirmed the dates as being significant, or that events did indeed occur.

Sometimes, giving a message to a colleague could be uncomfortable. Knowing information about your colleagues and having to tell them what you know, courtesy of spirit, could be a little tricky at times. It also put me in a high position of trust. This was not a problem since I earned their trust. My philosophy has always been that if someone has shared a problem with me, it doesn't belong to me, nor does it belong to anyone else.

Because my colleagues could trust me it didn't take long before I got the luncheon invitations. I didn't mind accepting the invitations, or doing readings, but I did have to limit the amount of lunchtime readings, especially since I hardly ever got to have a lunch hour. It would have been so easy for me to open up and run my office for the purpose of tarot and psychic readings. There would never be any shortage of clients!

Initially, it was extremely difficult to balance the demands between requests for readings and my work. Both proved to be a struggle; both were a full time job. There were many times I was not able to do a reading for someone, which I knew would disappoint them. I always tried to avoid disappointing people. I know only too well the meaning of disappointment; I had had my fair share over the years. Instead, I found and structured a balance that would not interfere with my work. I made both the demands of the job and requests for tarot and psychic readings work, even if it was exhausting to combine both!

One psychic reading I did for a colleague over a lunch time bothered me. I had gone into a state of semi-trance, unintentionally, and given her a message from spirit. After the reading had finished she asked me if I was alright. I didn't know what she meant until she told me my eyes had changed and my voice was not my own. I told her I was fine and was perhaps overcome with emotion transferred from the energy of the spirit. I didn't want to cause her any alarm. I didn't know who was more alarmed actually, me or my colleague.

Since I had the opportunity to work alongside many colleagues with different talents I always learned something new. I always enjoyed my work and working with others too. However, there was no one else other than Professor Paul that I enjoyed working for. I would work as his Personal Assistant for almost six years. It became the most enjoyable and satisfying role I had ever had. I found him to be very challenging, in a nice way.

The Professor used to be Dean of a faculty until his retirement was brought forward by Parkinson's disease. In his book he is currently writing he says of me, *'She can appear to be not with it and just a dumb blonde, but a little observation easily uncovers greater depth. She is also a fairly unique character, a sense of humour, (when things are going wrong she announces she is having a blonde day today). Although I do not know what to make of her sixth sense, I am sure she has some abilities beyond my comprehension, and since I know that what I do not know far exceeds my little knowledge, she comes into the unknown region comfortably for me. We have worked together a little on this and will continue to do so.'(Paul, R.J, 2008).* He hit the nail on the head when he said, 'She can appear to be not with it.' When you try to combine your mental functions on two dimensions, it can be a little busy!

Working at a Higher Education establishment I should have had qualifications equivalent to 'A' or 'O' levels and perhaps one or two GCSE's. But, I had nothing equivalent to any of these. The only thing I could offer was my own personal style of secretarial experience. I was a 'temp' when I first started working for Professor Paul. It was new and nerve racking to be in the company of a scientist, especially with my alternative talent. I felt I didn't deserve such a high profile role since there were others with far better qualifications. It also frightened me because of his status, but I learnt we are all human no matter what status a person has - nobody needs to be treated any differently.

I learnt this difference when I worked for the Professor. At one point I offered him the option of replacing me. I was open and honest when I told him I thought he deserved someone more 'qualified', but he wouldn't hear of it. I was glad my request fell on deaf ears so to speak because he has been my mentor and colleague for many years. He would often remind me 'if you don't believe you will succeed, you will succeed in your own belief.' I often try to succeed, but someone somewhere will always be there to put me down. Whether the knock down is healthy or not, it always makes me a stronger person.

Before the Professor invited me to work for him a second time, and in between contracts, I had been working as a Personal Assistant to a Pro-Vice Chancellor. I even had my own little office. I was glad I had an office to make my own. People would often comment on how they liked the feel of it, since it always appeared cosy and calm to them. I was also glad to have my own office because being 'sensitive' to other people's emotions could be sometimes draining. If a person was sad, annoyed or generally tired I would feel the same way. My own office was perfect!

When the opportunity arose for me to work for Professor Paul again I didn't hesitate. He knew of my ability but never asked me to prove myself; it didn't matter since his belief was different to mine. In fact, no one actually asked me to prove myself at all as a 'medium', which I suppose was a good thing.

Professor Paul's office was situated in an old building which at one time used to be a hospital. I never really fancied working in the building because it was not really centre to the hub of the institute. It had a feeling of separation from the other buildings. Whilst I had got to know many people, I didn't know many people in this building. I had visions of being kept busy, not only from the 'living', but of course there were those too!

As I expected, there were times when I was not alone in my new surroundings. I would experience a few things I cannot mention for fear of causing alarm. Nothing bad, but some people just wouldn't appreciate being told there was a ghost standing close to them. I was never surprised when people told me of experiencing strange phenomena in this building. A few colleagues would tell me how uncomfortable they felt. It was not because of me being there you understand, but because of the eerie feeling within the building, especially at night. There were things happening that could not be logically explained, footsteps in the dark for one, Oops! I liked this building.

The first day I worked in my new office proved to be eventful, but only because I was clumsy, nothing paranormal about that! I had been given a bunch of keys to the locks on my office and the two other offices adjacent to mine. One of the offices belonged to Professor Paul; the other accommodated three other colleagues.

I thought all was going well after the first hour until I returned from collecting the post, I found the keys wouldn't open the door. My colleague on arrival told me I shouldn't have dropped the latch on the door because there was no key to the lock. It could only happen to me, we were all locked out. Maintenance had to be called to fix the lock.

As if that wasn't impressive enough my second day also proved to be 'entertaining.' I made a pot of hot tea placing it on a tray with nice cups and saucers ready to serve to the Professor. But, before I had stepped into his office I managed to drop the tray all over the nice carpet smashing the tea service as it hit the floor. I suppose I should have realised cups and saucers never last long with me. I thought working in this office I could see how much of a smashing time I would have. I also thought 'things could only get better', well, you can think that can't you, and things did get better. I knew I would love working in my new office. Haunted or not!

My Spirit Guide, Hannah

Many weeks had passed after sacking Hannah, which left me feeling guilty. I had to apologise and ask her and the team of spirit guides (if there was a team) to come back. I realised it was my fault not theirs I had been unable to control spirit. I was totally to blame. I used to think my guides, especially Hannah would protect me. I was wrong; there was only so much they could do, the rest I had to do myself.

Hannah told me I wasn't listening to her, that I needed to see what I saw so I wouldn't be frightened of any spirit entity. She also told me she wanted to see how I would react at seeing spirit of all shapes, sizes and forms. She wanted to see if I was ready to do the real work. It was a test to see if I would sink or swim. I swam but not before almost drowning. I had to find my own lifebelt. Working with spirit is so easy and so beautiful, if you know how.

I have already mentioned in my first two years as a developing psychic I'd never met my spirit guide in a physical sense, nor was I aware I had such a thing as a spirit guide. I had got used to hearing the voice of a woman talking me; I didn't connect the voice to being that of my spirit guide, Hannah. People kept talking about theirs and a Spiritualist medium on TV kept talking to his. I thought at the time how silly and stupid he looked to keep turning round and speaking to someone no one else could see.

I was of the impression I didn't have a guide, one had never shown itself to me. I thought only people who were born psychic would be privileged to have a spirit guide. I always thought that perhaps if I turned around a guide would be there; or if I opened and closed my eyes one would appear. I remember thinking on many occasions, 'I want one of those, how do you get one? Can I nick his off TV?' Silly me, I didn't need his as I already had one but didn't know what to do with it.

Hannah served as a nurse in the Crimean war which would become so significant to me. I can't believe how significant in this life that war was. The place I worked in had a building named after another famous nurse in the very same war. I don't mind telling you that I dreamed of that place before the building existed, and before the name of the building was chosen!

Over the years Hannah has become my best friend and I am truly blessed to have such a highly evolved spiritual being by my side. I was pretty naïve in my early years to think I had been appointed a personal, highly evolved spiritual entity. But, as time went by I got talking to Hannah quite a bit. I can't say I am demanding of her, quite the contrary, more a case of if you're there all well and good, if not nothing I can do but I'll have a natter to you anyway. I would talk to her quite a bit. It was strange on the face of it how I would appear to be talking to myself. It took some getting used to, but once I did, holding conversations with an invisible person whilst talking out loud or in my mind became a doddle – no matter how stupid it looked!

During some of our chattettes I would test Hannah out to see if she came up with the right answers to questions I asked. I would ask and listen intently to see what answers she would give back. I would practice this method by standing next to people at work and ask Hannah for dates connected to them, or someone they knew they could identify with. The answer would come back and I would ask the person I was with if the information was significant to them. The accurate evidence usually spoke for itself.

I'm not perfect and don't claim to be, I can have my 'off' days just as other people have theirs, that's what makes me human. I would like to be 'spot on' all the time but it doesn't always happen. What does happen though is that when I am 'spot on' people look amazed or even stunned when I have told them something of significance. What they find amazing is my ability to accurately give dates, months and years relating to both the 'dead' and the 'living'.

I used to tell people names of their deceased loved ones and describe them when they stood beside me. I would tell them their loved ones hadn't died at all and that they wouldn't want them to think of them as 'dead' and gone. More like they were 'alive' and 'well' and a living spirit in the spirit world. That was my belief anyway; it was up to them if they shared the same belief, or to accept/reject the information given.

It didn't matter where I was, if spirit wanted to speak to me they would. They could and would, sometimes they would talk to me through my writing. Spiritual communication is not limited in any shape or form, quite the opposite actually. If spirit wanted to pass a message on they would find a way. I would receive emails from people all over the globe and without me realising it, Hannah, or spirit would be looking over my shoulder reading the same as I was reading.

If I was reading a mail sent from someone, Hannah, or a spirit person would tell me things relevant to the person sending the mail. This way I got to develop my psychic written skills and developed my psychic intuition further. Whenever there was a message to give I would just pop the message on at the end of the mail. I didn't want spirit to miss an opportunity. Nonetheless, I was always surprised when the person replied with a 'thank you', the message meant a lot to them and how incredibly accurate the information would be.

I can't explain why I predict future events, only that I know I can through the voices I hear. I know I can because people tell me I can. Sometimes I am not aware of what the event may be connected to, only that something of great significance will occur on a specific day.

I can't tell you how it all works only that it does, and only if you have faith and believe. I have experienced and learnt a great deal from Hannah. Although it's safe to say I am not the best communicator in the world, nor am I the best receiver of communications, from the living or the 'dead.' There are times when I don't understand everything, or understand everything but in a different context.

Working with spirit guides and spirit is like mastering an art, there is no art harder to master than that of patience. I learned how to be patient, not overnight granted, and I found it quite hard. It had its rewards though because patience led me to become a calmer person, once I got the gist of it! You can't rush spirit no matter how much you try; they have all the time in the world. Time is of no consequence in the spirit world, it doesn't exist, it is one period of time in one mass of space.

I learnt the hard way in that I had to be totally focused and ready for anything I was to learn from Hannah. She could be hard work my Hannah, or was it me taking two steps back instead of two steps forward! There are no short cuts in learning and meditation was a large part of my training.

People used to tell me to 'meditate', me, meditate, yeah right! Where would I find time to perform such a chore? I'm not the type of person who can keep still since my mind is always busy thinking. Usually about rubbish but it remains very active! Still, meditation would be a daft thing to do, or so I used to think. I wouldn't or couldn't meditate for the life of me but I could get used to relaxing. Relaxation seemed a better option; I could give that a bit of a go.

I'd psyche myself up before I attempted to relax, sometimes worn out from thinking about it! However, if this method was allegedly a better way of getting to know your spirit guide I was all for it. Nonetheless, I didn't know what to expect, but then neither did Hannah. I knew I was going to be hopeless.

Drawing the bedroom curtains and laying on my bed, CD player beside me I found some relaxing music. I was bored before I started! The first few times I tried it I would get so annoyed with myself because after only a few minutes I'd fall asleep. It was hard work trying to stay awake. I had to really discipline myself to behave and at least try, if only to stay awake.

The sound of angel music blasting out through my headphones sounded like heaven, but I couldn't relax. I would focus on what I wanted for dinner, what my next day at work would be like, should I buy new net curtains or change the wallpaper? The list was never ending. By the time I'd sorted out what I wanted for dinner, dumped the idea of purchasing new nets and pondered over what colour wallpaper to get, the ten minutes I'd allocated was up. Was it a waste of time? Absolutely not, I made more decisions in those ten minutes than I had thinking about the same things all day.

I repeated this process over many days and found I was thinking less of what I needed and more on getting to know my spirit guide. I learnt to relax my body if not my mind and began to speak to Hannah through my thoughts. I would feel a wisp of gentle cold air as she came close. I set aside some time each night for me and Hannah to interact, each time I would make the sessions last a little longer, each time I would get more out of the session. It was good.

I got to know more about Hannah and what type of person she was in her physical life. I was able to get quite a substantial amount of information that I wouldn't have got if I hadn't learnt to meditate. I still dislike that word, it gives me the 'eebie geebies', or creeps if you don't know what eebie geebies are.

Some people have told me they eat, sleep and work with their spirit guides 24/7. I find this hardly likely as spirit, like us, are energy forms. We are both life forms but function in different dimensions. Because we are life forms we both require replenishment in energy. We, as 'physical' beings, have the option of sleeping; whilst spirit has the option of resting whilst we sleep. Spirit, bless them do need a break, just as much as we do. Besides to have someone with you 24/7 would get on your nerves, wouldn't it?

I only call Hannah by my side when I am doing spiritual work, meditating, or when I need to know something. If I don't call her, she calls me if she feels I need to know something. Whilst Hannah may not be with me 24/7 she still has access to my thoughts and will let me know things, mostly on a need to know basis.

Getting to know your spirit guide can be frustrating, especially if you want to see who is guiding you. People often ask me why they can't see their spirit guide, and the only answer I can offer is that if a guide wants you to see them they will find a way for you to do so. But, if they don't then that's their choice, not yours. It's common though for a guide or a spirit for that matter to appear in the form of a glowing light, orb, sphere, coloured light, twinkling lights or even a light anomaly.

You have to keep working with your guide in order to achieve that special bond between you. I got into a routine of making a regular date with Hannah; I made time for us both to get to know one another better. The more I got to know her the more I accepted her as my spirit guide, I'm sure some people accept anyone, I nearly did!

I guess it's similar to a relationship you would have on the earth plane with a physical person. The more you get to know them the more you can get to like them. I made the commitment to work with Hannah and found my own way of blending with her. Mind you, at first I had no idea how it all worked, as it happens I thought I had been doing all the work by myself.

I tried different ways and different techniques of working with Hannah and wasn't really fussed, at first that is. I did remind her that I was the one in control of working with her and spirit, not her, or any other type of spirit. I wasn't going through all that madness again, no thank you! Finding out how to best work with your spirit guide is done by practicing.

Practicing doesn't mean every other month when it's convenient for you, or to call on your guide because you need an answer to a pressing question. I mean practice by daily workouts with your spirit guide. Instead of going to the gym, get in touch with the spirit world, it's a lot less energetic and a whole lot cheaper, well, actually it's free.

Keep talking, keep asking and keep the energy vibration flowing and building up between both of you. If you can persevere and keep the vibration patterns between you and your guide going you will learn to trust. Make a note of the word 'trust' as it will always feature high on your list. If you want to learn how to be a spiritual interpreter and pass on messages to recipients you will need 'trust' as a tool. Believe me, once you have mastered this tool it will help you gain and use a new found confidence you thought you never had. It worked for me!

It worked so well for me, this word called 'trust.' I would sit at my computer in a psychic chat room attempting to give a message to someone. I always knew when someone in the spirit world was close to me as I would hear a voice. As I heard their voice I would start typing words in the little chat box. Except, I would type in something completely different, I lacked confidence. I hadn't listened to my guide, I took the second or third word that I heard and it would be wrong. It was wrong because it was my word and not spirits, a lesson to be learnt. I should have trusted my guide and gone with the first word or image heard or shown.

It was having the confidence to give the word I heard even if it seemed frightening to me. How could I give it when it didn't look as though it would make sense? Or I may be wrong? So, why didn't I give the first word? Simple, I had a fear of being wrong when my fear should have been about being right. This taught me a big lesson, I had to give what my guide or spirit gave first, anything else would be nonsense. If I didn't hear anything, which was very rare, I wouldn't have anything to give. If I had nothing to give I'd have to disappoint the person, better to disappoint than talk nonsense!

Learning to interpret words, symbols and visions wasn't easy. It's a bit like being back in nursery school where the teacher writes on a blackboard or holds up a drawing. You have to pay close attention to what is being transmitted. For instance, and a good example is when I was doing a reading on the Internet, Hannah repeated a particular name not once but twice, not one name but two. I felt really reluctant to type the names in the chat box. However, when I heard her say 'Trust me.' I thought, 'Sod it, I'm with you luvvie, I'm going along with what your telling me, nothing to lose,' and typed in the names she had given me. I trusted her 100% and she knew this.

I could feel the hair standing up on the back of my neck as I typed in the names, 'Donna Alexandra'. I felt the coldness of someone standing close to me as I waited for the reply to come back from the person, who would be sitting somewhere in the world on another computer. I was nervous to say the least as I didn't know what to expect, except that I may be talking complete nonsense to this woman I had just met in the chat room; a woman who didn't know me from Adam.

The words blew the woman away, as I looked up and read on the screen I saw the woman's reply; 'it's my daughter, that's my daughter's first and middle name.' I was like, 'Wow Hannah.' I blew her a huge kiss and whispered, 'Thank you.' I had tears running down my face. I turned to the spirit girl who had appeared to the side of me and said, 'you're ok darling, your mum knows your here'.

So, for those of you who want to make up words as you go along, forget it, you won't come out shining. Stick with what you hear the first time round from spirit, or your spirit guide. By doing this you're reading will hold credible validation to you and the person for whom you are reading. It will also please your guide to know you have learned to 'trust'.

Asking Hannah once if I could work the same way as the American medium John Edward, my request was granted. I found myself being shown the title of TV programmes, people in the TV programmes, objects and other things. It was hilarious to work this way but it wasn't working for me when I tried reading in the Internet chat room. I was hopeless with TV trivia. I was going round in circles trying to explain a programme I had no knowledge of. It was working but it really wasn't the way I wanted to work. I soon asked Hannah to change the way we worked back to our own normality, she complied with my request, thankfully. Bless her.

Haunted Messages

The haunted messages I have received from spirits have been heart-breaking, loving, amusing, touching, but most of all comforting. Above all, the voices and the messages I have given from spirit have been truthful. I have taken some of these 'haunted messages' and written them here because I know I will never forget them. I know too that the 'haunted messages' will also be a memory to those who received them.

Messages from the 'dead' have been communicated to me through a wide variety, and sometimes unusual method. The voice and presence of spirit has helped me to interpret their messages through face to face readings, Internet readings, workshops, circles, charity functions, demonstrations in halls, church platform, séances, email, teaching television and paranormal investigations.

Within the diversity of work I have undertaken, I have gained a deeper understanding of spirit, ghosts and the 'dead.' I have also gained a wealth of experience and understanding of 'The Living' too. No one can understand the heartbreak a death can bring to a person, family, friend or colleague unless they themselves have experienced a loss. A loss is not something to be described with ease; it is something that is felt through an abundance of divine love.

I have experienced many close family losses but it wasn't until many years later, and following my sister's death that I became interested in the soul's survival and the survival of consciousness. I always knew my sister was with me but didn't know how to communicate with her. I didn't even know if I could talk to her. My need to keep her close led me to visit Spiritual churches.

I went to church in the hope my sister would make contact with me through the medium. Although I never heard from her at church I was never disappointed, I knew there were others who needed messages more than me. Besides, I knew my sister was very much around me because I always felt her closeness.

I had been told by different mediums many times that I would be working on the church platform. I thought at the time they must have mixed me up with someone else since it wasn't one of my ambitions. I didn't mind giving messages to people at church but always over a cup of tea and a biscuit.

The secretary at one church was so impressed with the accuracy of a message I gave her she invited me to work on the platform. I didn't like to refuse, and so I agreed. Turning up on my night I was nervous; it wasn't like I was demonstrating the latest lipstick or broomstick; I would be demonstrating messages from loved ones in spirit. Spirits only I could see and hear. I knew I would only be as good as spirit were and this would be a test for us both.

I was nervous but confident; the demonstrations were going really well and I was giving beautiful messages. I was making sense and spirit was making sense until one spirit interrupted my flow. Well, there's always one isn't there! I knew I should have told her to go away because of her energy and tone, but I didn't. This lady could easily have got me into trouble, or got someone in trouble for what I revealed. I found myself tip-toeing around the message I had to give out.

Being overly pushy, the spirit asked me to go to the lady in the front row. The lady in the front row was sitting with a man, nothing unusual there, probably her husband or partner. However, because of the spirit lady's energy I felt her message would not be so gratefully received.

Anyway, there was I, stood centre stage, (story of my life) with an angry spirit whom I dared not work with. I went full steam ahead smiling and giving the woman in the front row a message. I gave a few names and a few dates amongst other things and got nods of acknowledgement back in return.

The nods soon stopped the more I got into the reading and whilst I like people to say, 'No,' if I interpret the message wrong, I knew this woman should have been saying, 'Yes.' I began to feel the woman didn't really want to be the recipient of the message. However, I was sure the information I was receiving was true and it didn't seem that bad. Well, not at the start.

After a few more 'No's' I checked back with the spirit lady that what she was telling me was right and asked my guide for double confirmation. I felt something was very wrong with this message and wanted to call a stop to it. The woman in the front row was not looking at me at all and her eyes were fixed firmly on the floor. Her partner was looking at me intrigued but for some reason I really wanted to avoid him. I was irritated the woman kept looking at the floor.

Everyone was looking at me as though I didn't know what to say, they would have been right, I didn't. I began to feel a bit uncomfortable to say the least. I checked back with the spirit lady telling her I wasn't making sense, she wasn't making sense. I told her I was not comfortable with what she was giving me. I told her perhaps I had got the wrong person. I even thought another spirit had come in and the message was for someone else. Spirit can do that, change energies round.

The spirit lady made it quite clear the message was right and that I was with the right person. After she shouted in my ear, 'She knows darn well it's all for her, she's *bleep* having an affair and that's my son she's married to. I want him to know!' I wanted the floor to open up underneath me.

I stood there wondering how I could give this information to the woman now sitting nervously in front of me. I wondered if I could or should tell her. Could I tell her in front of her partner and everyone else what I had been told? 'Nah, absolutely not, don't be daft.' I coughed a few times, thanked the spirit for visiting and told the lady sitting in the front row how sorry I was she didn't understand the message. I left her mother-in-law's … love … cough ... and not so many blessings with her.

Not one to be put off by the 'unknown' I accepted another invitation to do an evening of private readings at another church. This time I would take along my tarot cards, I often read the cards and allow spirit to communicate should they choose. Arriving at the church, I settled down into a hard uncomfortable chair and got my tarot cards out placing them on the table. Before I had finished setting up my table a lady came over and sat in the chair directly opposite me. As she sat down I smiled at her as I became aware of a gentleman standing by the side of her.

The reading started off really well which is always good and I proceeded in giving names, dates, years along with other events. The lady smiled acknowledging a 'yes' to what I was saying. I wasn't a hundred percent sure she should be the recipient of the message; whilst it made sense, I didn't feel it was meant for her. I had to ask her, 'Were you supposed to come with a friend tonight who didn't come?' She replied, 'Yes, my friend was coming but pulled out at the last minute'.

My feelings were right, the message wasn't for her but instead spirit intended her to be the recipient of the message for someone close to her. I told her, 'The message is for your friend and not you.' She replied saying, 'Yes, it is all for her, I knew she should have come, everything you have said relates to her husband in spirit. I didn't want you to stop because I wanted him to finish before I told you.' Spirit has proved that they can work in mysterious ways.

The way spirit work is always a mystery, not just to me but others too. So when I demonstrated at another public engagement it gave me the opportunity to remind a lady of her grandmother's anniversary. The lady was slightly embarrassed, not so much that she could not take the date I gave, well, not at first that is, but more embarrassed that she had forgotten and the anniversary of her grandmothers passing would be in two days time. I let her and the audience know that a little 'haunted message' is all it takes from spirit to remind us of their existence.

Sometimes messages do haunt me, especially if I remember them well. There were times when I wished I didn't remember. I couldn't say no to my friend Deanna when she asked if I could do a reading for her daughter Adrianna. Her daughter wanted to know when she would meet her soul mate. During the reading I listened to spirit and gave her the name of a man she would meet. She met the man whose name I had given in the reading whilst on holiday, in another country. As much as I'd like to say they lived happily ever after, he was just a passing friend and their relationship ceased.

After I finished Adrianna's reading she asked if I would read for her mum. I didn't mind as there were still a few spirits standing in the corner waiting for their turn. I didn't want the spirits to stay all night; I'd had a long day. I got used to working with symbols and images but nothing could have prepared me for what I was about to receive. One spirit related to Deanna came and stood next to me. I wasn't truly thankful either when he started with his communication. Apart from giving his name, he was gracious to present me with a pair of mans genitals as an image. These 'bits' that were dangling in front of me caused me to do a double take, just to make sure I wasn't seeing things. I wasn't!

I wondered how on earth I could explain this. I always like to give what I get but this was a little ... naughty and a little tricky. I tried to conceal my laughter as I told Deanna what I was seeing, she burst out laughing. Much to her disappointment she wasn't able to see what I saw. I tried to keep a straight face as I checked with the spirit man the purpose of these well rounded balls, at the same time not really wanting an answer, I think. I kept these 'bits' in my sight for a while longer as you do. Then, it suddenly became clear why his 'bit's were of significance. On one of his 'bits' appeared the number 2 and on the other the number 22. I asked Deanna if these numbers meant anything to her. Well, you could have knocked her over with a feather as her jaw dropped. Short of picking her up off the floor she told me she lived at number 2 before moving to her current house, number 22.

I had no idea where she currently lived or lived before, nor did I know that the numbers would be significant. I had no reason to know. She explained to me that her husband also did those two numbers in the lottery. Perhaps I should have asked spirit for more balls!

The lottery numbers are something spirit will not give us. If only! I'm not even going to go there and try to explain why I haven't got a huge mansion, a Mercedes convertible or on permanent holiday.

I can be good with numbers when used in dates as my next 'haunted message' will demonstrate. An old friend of mine, Jack, sent me an email to tell of his unwanted but pending redundancy. When I replied back to him I told him not to worry and that the number five would be significant. He emailed me shortly after I gave him this information to tell me he had applied for a job, had an interview on the fifth and was appointed the position.

I'm often surprised to hear from people who remember a date I predict for them and that the date was of significance. The common view is that some old grey haired lady visits the hairdressers on a weekly basis is the image of the spirit, a grandmother type of such little distinction, she could be anyone's grandmother, mine included! When I can use dates together with a description of the spirit then that for me is confirmation enough.

Confirmation of another date that was remembered and proved to be significant was after a sitting with Perry, a PhD student. He emailed me after checking a date with his father to tell me I had been 'spot on.' In his mail he wrote 'I spoke to my dad to find out about the number 18 that you had mentioned relating to a guardian spirit in the other realm. 18th November is the date my grandmother died. The astrologers my parents have consulted in India in the last year have indicated exactly the same as you regarding my question. Your reading affirmed a lot of their observations; it almost mirrors what they have said. I actually found this quite astonishing given that we come from completely different cultural backgrounds. I have also started to focus back on my PhD and have started to set new deadlines to finish the first draft by this April. So, April you mentioned also becomes quite significant to me.' I was pleased Perry found the message so encouraging, once he had checked the date of his grandmother's passing.

No check was needed when a Professor from a leading London University came to visit a colleague of mine. He had come to act as an external examiner for one of the PhD students. He had also enquired if I could give him a psychic and tarot reading. Well, I nearly fell off my chair; it was such a strange request. I didn't mind though and was only too pleased to oblige.

As soon as he sat down next to me I told him I was aware of a female energy standing close to him. I gave the names of 'Marianna' and 'Glenda', at the same time felt they were being given to me twice. Both the names belonged to his late grandmother. One of the names also belonged to his wife, the other to his sister-in-law who was visiting his wife. I told him of a year that was significant to him. The year was significant because he had graduated. I continued to tell him a specific date and month that was significant to him. He accepted the information to be the exact date and month of his late father's birthday.

The reading went really well and he was very pleased. I am also pleased to report I have been superficially 'scientifically' tested under 'natural' conditions! The conditions couldn't have been more 'natural'. I'm no stranger to reading for academics in natural conditions though; it's almost part of an expected routine for me.

Sometimes dates can bring immense joy and happiness too. So, when Sandra, a friend of mine brought her colleague Elaine to see me I didn't know how the reading would go. Similarly, Elaine didn't know herself what the outcome would be. I did know during the reading how fed up and lonely Elaine was. She had no one to share her life with. I couldn't ignore the voice I heard telling me she would meet a man on a certain date on a certain month. I gave her the information to take away with her. Months later Sandra called to tell me of Elaine's engagement; it was on the exact date and month I had predicted. Sadly, she didn't stay with him too long after the engagement. But, for a while it did bring her the happiness she needed.

Haunted Internet

I used to engage in many conversations with many people over the Internet. Mostly conversing with people I had never met. The Internet would be my platform for working with spirit and for me to give messages to people. It was the place where my spiritual name of *'Goldy'* was born. It happened when I was desperate to get into a chat room on a psychic site but needed to register.

I thought registering would be easy seeing as the chat room was very new, I thought wrong. Every time I entered my real name a message would come back telling me it was 'unavailable'. After trying a variety of names close to that of my own the same message would come back 'unavailable'. I was just about to give up when a voice whispered 'Goldy'. I'd never heard the name before and it certainly didn't sound anything like my own name, but I typed it in nonetheless. To my astonishment I was accepted, had access and was in!

I visited the same room every night for months on end but decided I would build my own website and install my own chat room, which I successfully ran for four years. People would pass through either for spiritual readings or to learn, sometimes visit to share a problem. Whatever their reason for coming, I knew I would be helping them. If I couldn't help them then there was always someone somewhere who could.

The people I was communicating spiritual messages to helped me to understand more about the way spirit work. I got used to spirit showing me symbols, referring to TV programmes, giving me calendar dates and showing me images. All these metaphors helped towards developing my psychic ability and paving the way for my mediumistic skills to strengthen.

I would sit at the computer night after night in my psychic chat room talking to people who became my extended circle of friends. Chatting to people over the Internet seemed weird at first. I always thought people had to be sat in front of you to have a reading. This wasn't the case because the voices from beyond the grave would be with me, wherever I was.

It was the voice of spirit I would hear, the voice of a dead person speaking to me. Only they weren't dead, they wanted me to speak to their loved ones who were on the other end of the computer speaking to me.

If I hadn't known the person I was communicating with, or had any knowledge of them, or knew anyone connected to them, how come I knew so much about them? I knew because the voice of spirit knew the recipient of the message. I knew because it was the spirits' way of letting me know they were still alive and still watching over those who could not physically see them. I knew because I trusted spirit and my spirit guide, Hannah.

I don't know where my energy came from but at night I would tap away for hours on my laptop computer whilst in bed. I would be engrossed in working with the spirits that came to give messages to those I would be talking (typing) to. So engrossed was I one night in a reading I was doing, I didn't hear Hubby come in from work. It wasn't until I glanced up and saw him walk through the bedroom door I realised he was home. As he walked in the room he said, 'Hello luv, did you have a nice night?' Reaching over the bed he kissed me on the cheek before taking his jacket off and placing it on the chair.

I continued with the reading and tapped away on my computer as I listened to Hubby at the same time, or I thought I was. I was aware of his presence but was too focused on the reading to hold a conversation with him. It wasn't until I looked up I realised he had already gone downstairs. Twenty minutes later I also realised Hubby hadn't brought me up a cup of tea which was unusual. I was just about to finish the reading when Hubby walked into the room. He reached over the bed, kissed me on the cheek and took his jacket off, placing it on the chair.

Forgive me here if I seem confused but it was a bit like *déjà vu*. I asked Hubby why he had gone through the same routine again, kissed me, took his jacket off, placed it on the chair and not made me a cuppa. He said he had just got home! We argued jokingly about it but he was sticking by what he said and wasn't budging. He stuck by the fact he had just got home and that he had not walked into the room earlier. I stuck by my facts too. Sometimes I suppose you have to accept the here and now and sometimes the past, present and future.

After four years I closed my site down, I wanted to learn more spiritually and couldn't do it whilst my website was active. There were plenty of other sites to visit, so when I was able I visited another friend of mine Tracey's psychic chat room. It was a nice place for me to chill out and relax. It was not unusual for me to be in the chat room and have my list of MSN people in the corner of my computer screen showing, I could chat to my friends in between the room readings that spirit were keeping me busy with.

It was probably a big mistake having my MSN on at the same time as I was in the psychic chat room. But, whilst not conversing with anyone on MSN since my focus was in the chat room I became a bit puzzled when a spirit man came and stood by my side. I described him to the room but no one could own him. I decided to browse down the list of names in my MSN to see who was on line when I felt drawn to Jackie. I had known Jackie for a short time as a visitor to her site but didn't really know much about her. I asked the spirit man if Jackie was the person he wanted to make contact with to which he replied 'Yes'.

I clicked on Jackie's name and asked her if she knew a man who smoked a pipe, dressed in grey and wore a heavy jacket and trilby hat. She replied 'what age do you see him as'. I replied 'probably in his 70's, has a moustache and calls himself 'Len' or 'Lennie'. Jackie replied 'oh yes, I got an uncle that age, Len was Lenny'. I looked at the spirit man and saw him smiling. I smiled back at him and was happy I had found the person he had come for. Although I was totally perplexed as to why he should make contact with someone I wasn't actually having a conversation with.

I continued to tell Jackie he was talking about 'Windermere' and asked her if it meant anything; I felt it was connected to the name of a road. She replied 'Windermere Lane does actually'. I told her Lenny was telling me he used to tell 'porky pies' (lies). Jackie relied 'Yes, there's a famous one'. The energy changed as I felt a new energy come forward. I was aware of another man standing by my side and asked him what his name was and he replied 'Arthur'. I asked him 'Are you here for Jackie too?' He replied 'Yes', so I asked Jackie if she knew Arthur but she couldn't recall one. Arthur wanted me to remember Bertha to her who was also in spirit. I asked Jackie if Bertha was a name she could take in the spirit world, she replied 'yes, that's a name I haven't thought about for years'.

I could feel the energy of Bertha come closer and felt happy with this spirit, she was a nice lady with not a care in the world. Bertha told me the year 1969 was significant to Jackie so I asked her 'Is 1969 significant to you Jackie, feel it's an important date'. Jackie replied 'Yes, very'. Bertha went on to tell more and I relayed our conversation to Jackie telling her; 'Bertha tells me she liked bingo and was a bit of a dolly bird, blue shirts is all she used to iron and housework would be never ending for her, is that right?'. Jackie relied 'yes, makes sense'. I said 'Bertha also wants to remember Terry and Meg, a family who had four brothers and a sister, does this make sense?' Jackie replied 'Yes, that's dad family, I remember

79

Meg'. I said 'Ok, she's telling me 2001 is very significant to you, would you understand?' Jackie replied 'Yes, I got divorced'.

Over the years I have been working with spirits I now know why months, dates and years are significant to people and I know too that spirit were there to witness or predict the events. Bertha told me everything would come out smelling of roses for Jackie so I typed this in the message and Jackie replied 'You know it was always one of her sayings'.

I was pleased these spirits dropped in and I was able to give Jackie confirmation of their existence in the spirit world. I was also pleased spirit guided me to her name as quite a lot of significant and personal details came out. Because of the visitations from spirit Jackie told me how she felt a lot better than she had been recently feeling. I was just about to close the conversation when I heard the soft voice of a spirit lady give her name as 'Tracey'. I was beginning to think Jackie had an army of spirit over on the other side. I asked Tracey if she was visiting for Jackie too, as I anticipated her reply, she said 'Yes'. I had a feeling I hadn't finished.

Catching Jackie before she went I sent her another message telling her I didn't think we were finished and would she understand the name 'Tracey'. Jackie replied 'Yes, not a person I was keen on'. I thought 'Oops' best not get involved with this one apologised to Tracey and asked her to go back. As Tracey's energy went away I felt another energy come forward, still female, so asked if she was here for Jackie too. No surprise when she confirmed she was.

I continued with Jackie's reading and told her another lady had stepped in by the name of Irene. Jackie confirmed this lady was someone her mum knew and who was also in the spirit world. Irene was a little chatty, where she got the energy from I will never know but perhaps it was because there were so many spirits present. When many spirits are present they can share the mass amount of energies between them.

I told Jackie Irene claimed she loved fish and chips and felt this was very significant. Jackie replied 'Oh my God, fancy picking that up, yes, she had a chippie'. I told Jackie Irene had a stepson and I was to mention the name of 'Ronald'. Jackie replied 'Yes, she did have a stepson, and yes I have a brother I never met called Ronald'. Feeling sure this was to be the last message from Irene I thanked her and spirit once again. I thanked Jackie for receiving the messages with the love they came with. I was just about to close the window when a male energy came close to me, his energy was very strong.

Before I could finish saying my goodbye's to Jackie I said 'Hang on, got someone else here for you luvvie, do you know a man with his front teeth missing, had connections to Brid or Bridge Street and a Swan is of significance. He wore braces that he would tug and has a northern accent?' I felt if I didn't speak on this spirit mans behalf he may thump me so I said as much as I could with what he had given me, I just needed Jackie to reply. When she replied she said 'Yes big time, it was the Swan Pub in Bridge Street he is talking about'. I said 'He was a wheeler dealer man, always ready to make a bob or two in old cars, scrap metal or iron'. Jackie confirmed he was an iron merchant.

The party seemed to go on for hours with spirit popping in and out, anyone and everyone seemed to want to be remembered to Jackie. Even Larry, who I prayed would be the last, well almost but not quite! Larry was Jackie's cousin's boyfriend who had passed over into the spirit world. Larry had also brought through Trisha, a lady who belonged to her husband's side of the family. As I was receiving messages I told Jackie there were two brothers who were twins in the spirit world, the twins brought with them another spirit called Alfie.

Jackie was able to identify all the spirits with great ease and without hesitation and explained that Alfie and the twins were her Gran's brothers. Adding she had only been thinking about them that evening. I told Jackie she was also thinking about doing a boot sale; she was shocked I should know this as she had only been talking about it earlier on in the evening.

Spirit was going to keep me working so when Freddie stepped forward from the other side I had to continue. Jackie was not only amazed at the amount of spirit making the communications with her, she was also surprised I knew they were all for her. Freddie told me she would remember him if I was to say he was better known as 'Fairground Freddie'. I asked Jackie if she remembered a 'Fairground Freddie' to which she replied 'Yes, he was the last person I expected to be here'. Freddie gave the name of 'Dotty' which Jackie could also take as Freddie's mother.

Just when I thought I had finished the date of 27th March was given to me. Jackie confirmed this to be Freddie's wife's birthday. Alas, it didn't stop there. I saw the guy from the TV programme Cracker but I couldn't think of his name. I asked Jackie 'why would I be seeing the man from the programme 'Cracker'. She replied 'Robbie Coltrane is an actor and Coltrane was a family name on Freddie's side'. I told her he gave me the number 17 and that it was significant to her. Jackie replied '17th is my mum's birthday, next week'.

We still weren't finished, there was still more spirit to come. Not to be outdone by spirit a man with a glass eye giving the name of 'Tommy' appeared by the side of me. He claimed to be connected to a Chris. I asked Jackie if she knew Tommy in spirit. She replied 'Yes, Tommy is father in law in spirit, Chris is ex hubby'. Freddie also gave the name of Brenda and I gave it to Jackie, again asking if she could take this name to which the reply was 'Yes, it's his wife's sister'. The rest of the reading was of a personal nature relating to Jackie's family problems at the time. Because of this it is not possible to relay the rest of the spiritual messages.

The reading was done with great ease and great clarity from my side and the side of spirit. I was very pleased with myself and with spirit that I was able to convey the messages to Jackie. It made both, if not all of us very happy. I knew there were more spirit people with me, but I also knew I had to go to bed. I would have been there all night if spirit had their way! It was quite a party, the biggest 'Haunted Internet' on-line party I had ever had the privilege of being part of.

The Investigator

My own approach to ghost investigating, in practice, does not match how some programmes on TV portray it to be. It all looks very easy, and at times can appear to look quite over dramatic. Sitting watching a ghost investigating programme in the comfort of your own home is completely different to physically getting out there and doing it for yourself, as I was to discover.

I had never, prior to my own apprenticeship, investigated ghosts. I had no idea of what to expect, outside of fear that is. Fear used to be the first thing I'd experience in any situations I had with ghosts.

I used to think what would happen if I came face to face with a ghost, or what if I saw something floating in mid air? I would even think a ghost might jump out in front of me and scare me half to death. But, of course, none of that happened. It's pretty amazing what thoughts can do, I'd scared myself senseless before I even got anywhere. Besides, initially, apart from the ghosts, spirits and apparitions in my own house, I wasn't sure I wanted to meet anyone else's.

My relationship with ghosts and spirits over the years has been a two way affair, especially since I was virtually brought up with them. We've had a very productive love/hate relationship, only now its pure love. But, as a paranormal investigator, love it or loathe it, I didn't know quite how well I would fare.

I did have a bit of an advantage though investigating the paranormal because I could use my psychic senses. But, relying on senses alone wasn't going to improve my skills or conquer my fear. Like any other apprentice, I started at the bottom of the ladder and worked my way up.

I investigated haunted houses which were a good platform for me in the early years, the smaller the better. As the platform grew during my time spent as an apprentice, my ambitions would grow too. The houses increased in size, invitations came from bigger venues and battles began with bigger opportunities. There was no shortage of a haunting.

I didn't see myself as a 'Ghost Hunter' since I wasn't hunting ghosts. I abhor the name and find it an insult to the 'dead.' My intentions are never to hunt the 'dead', but to find out more about the 'dead.' I could only do this by investigating the 'dead' and the 'haunted' places I visited.

There were many visits to haunted places, together with many years of experimenting and hard work before I was competent in what I was doing. I didn't consider myself to be a 'professional' based on a few investigations alone. My professionalism came with experience; the more I got out there, the more I learnt. I couldn't have done it without the ghosts, spirits and my spirit guide. In education speak, I was engaged in work based learning.

But, before I could do the work as a paranormal research investigator I needed to face my fears. Perhaps easier said than done! However, I did confront all my fears and learnt very quickly that the 'dead' were only too willing to show they weren't 'dead.' This knowledge helped my work become my research, and my research become my work. Both offset one another.

My knowledge of the 'dead' came from my fear and battles I'd had with ghosts and spirits in my own house. However, a portion of my experience came from the battles I was to encounter in other people's homes. But my fears weren't just about what type of ghost, if any, I would face, but also about what type of place I would be invited to, or choose to investigate. I would be in 'unknown' territory.

Sometimes I had been invited to investigate a place because a ghost was causing problems and was no longer required. There were some places that enjoyed the 'services' of a ghost because it was good for business. Some places built their reputation on being haunted even if they weren't. If a place was known to be haunted I would be asked not to do anything to make the ghost leave. The ghost I would be told had to stay. This proved a bit of problem for me since everything is free will, as we all know. But, how do you tell a ghost who wants to cross over (return to the spirit world), 'Sorry mate you can't go because you're proving to be a nice little earner.' I will leave it to your imagination as to what I did, or didn't do!

Many buildings can speak to you just by observation alone. The bricks and mortar along with the décor would give clues as to its history, or even its use. Every building has a story to tell. Nonetheless, if a building had a ghost, or demonstrated paranormal phenomena it would be a nice little bonus. If I could use my psychic mind to receive communications from a ghost or a spirit and have it validated - it would be like winning the lottery!

A psychic mind is never enough, no matter what or how much information is received. People, including myself, always look for solid evidence. I found my evidence when I invested in the purchase of audio and visual equipment. I bought anything I could use to validate and support the possibility of a haunting.

My Hubby, bless him, supported me totally in my quest and bought me a night-vision cam-corder. I found some night vision colour spy cams on eBay and used them with our spare TV's. Voice recorders were a must so I bought quite a few. I purchased trigger objects that could be placed in different locations to monitor any anomalies. And, I bought toys for the ghosts of children. I bought anything that may prove useful in finding proof.

I found different forms of evidence through the amount of research my team had gathered. I used this evidence to form part of a preliminary or final report for the venue we investigated. Putting together a report for a project takes months of hard work, time and commitment. My time and dedication to all my projects proved to be well worth the effort.

I would build case studies through the analysis of team member reports, photographs, videos, camcorder tapes, EVP's (electronic voice phenomena), EMF (electro magnetic field) readings and temperature recordings. My social life was zero because I was always sifting through materials gathered after an investigation. I didn't mind though, I quite enjoyed the prospect of finding something I couldn't explain. But, I couldn't do anything with the evidence I had found and that was another battle. There is no professional body set up to examine paranormal evidence. Perhaps with the amount of proof people seem to be collecting the world over, an organisation may take an interest in sponsoring or funding such projects. On the other hand, it could be no one is interested in keeping a data base of evidence for fear of having to explain it!

I'm always interested as to why the paranormal is hard for some to accept when evidence has been witnessed, or experienced. It can be so easy for people to dismiss the possibility of the survival of death. Yet, I remember well one conversation I had with Professor Paul when I asked him the question, 'Why is it that people find it hard to accept the possibility of the soul's survival?' He said, 'Millions of people all over the world have, or will perhaps experience some form of phenomena that cannot be explained. Most of which will have a logical or reasonable explanation. Others will simply be aware that what has happened to them will be hard for the human mind to comprehend, therefore, will not pursue it further. The numerous witnesses to paranormal events would make it implausible for their stories to be dismissed without any form of further investigation.' I found this explanation to be as good as any reason I can think of.

If only we understood more about the paranormal and the Universe we live in, but we don't. There is too much information contained within it. Some will only accept the human race as one kind of phenomena that resides within it. But, just as the human race has their model of 'law and order', the Universe too has its own sequence of 'Fundamental Laws'.

We can accept that the Universe as a whole is a place where time and space exists, where we the human race exist. The difference being to the human mind is that nothing exists unless it is seen. Scientists for hundreds of years have been dismissing the possibility of life on other dimensions. The hypothesis being is that life cannot be extended beyond that of our own.

Beginners Luck

I never expected people to ask me to visit their home because of unexplained phenomena, or in other words, ghostly activity. So when I received an invitation to investigate a house that had an alleged 'ghost', I had to think long and hard before accepting such a strange invitation. It would be a challenge, true, but I hadn't investigated anyone else's house before, never mind someone else's ghost. I had enough of my own!

It was apparent that Gemma, whose house was behaving badly, was troubled. I thought it was very kind of her to invite me to investigate her rather somewhat 'troubled' house. But was it her house that was troubled I wondered? I was undecided.

I certainly didn't want to pass myself off as someone who knew what to do, or someone with a wealth of ghost investigating experience. I really didn't know how I could actually help with someone's unwanted ghost or spirit.

I thought for a few days about visiting this place before I finally and reluctantly agreed. I was open and honest as I reminded Gemma about my lack of experience. I told her I didn't know if I would really be of any use. She was not put off by my lack of enthusiasm and fully understood where I was coming from. She didn't seem to mind my lack of investigative experience. She was happy enough to know I talk to the 'dead.' It was the 'dead' she insisted was causing problems for her and her three housemates.

From my own experience, *we* can be the problem for those on the other side. Anyway, we made a date and I visited the property. I arrived at the house early evening whilst it was still light, a deliberation on my part since I didn't want to go in the dark. I was rather hoping no one was home as I stood in the porch and rang the door bell. My hopes were sunk when Gemma answered the door and led me through to the kitchen.

Sat huddled round the dining table were Gemma's three other housemates. We said our little jollies and I made a few jokes to put them at ease, or was I trying to put myself at ease. I didn't really know and wondered what the hell I was doing there. If I were to be totally honest, I didn't know who was more nervous, me or them. It should have been me but somehow I didn't think it was.

I'm not one to show my nerves, neither did I let my nerves show when I felt the coldness of a spirit energy stand next to me. This was good, they were definitely haunted. It didn't take me long to know I was in the presence of an elderly female spirit. Whoever she was, she was absolutely divine. She was no trouble. I felt really comfortable in her company and she made feel remarkably at ease. I didn't convey to the ladies about her presence at the time because I could see their fear. Besides, they would probably be frightened if I came out and said 'your ghost is here'!

I refrained from telling them anything as I walked round the house guided by the presence of the spirit lady. I was trying to hold a three way conversation, me talking to the spirit, the house mates talking to me, and me talking to the housemates. I can get confused having a two way conversation at times, let alone three! The housemates excitedly told me of events that had kept them awake at night. I had rather they hadn't! They told me how much they feared being in their own home. They had my sympathy. Gemma explained how they all slept in one room together as no one wanted to sleep alone. Apparently, they hadn't slept in their own rooms for many weeks. I still hadn't told them there was six of us now and not five.

I didn't mind the spirit lady walking with me, it seemed so natural. I wasn't the least bit worried. However, I couldn't wait to find out how they had all got to sleeping in one room, although I could easily relate to their reasons for doing so. It's far from easy sharing your home with the 'dead.

It happens though doesn't it? When you find out you're not alone, you need someone to give you a rational explanation to all the strange phenomena you have witnessed. I was that 'someone' who had some explaining to do on behalf of the spirit lady. She had become a little bit of a nuisance as she went about her business around the house. Only, she didn't realise she was a nuisance. I am sure she wouldn't have wanted to cause upset to the ladies of the house.

I began to get the picture as one of the women told me about the bathroom taps which would constantly run water. No matter how many times the taps were turned off the water would always run again. It didn't please them either to hear the sound of footsteps that paced the wooden floor at night. This was one of the main reasons they huddled up together in one room.

The footsteps would suddenly stop as they reached their bedroom door. Quietly and slowly the door knob would turn and the door would open. The women would shake and stay awake all night laden with fear. All the while I was talking to the spirit lady I knew I had some explaining to do, to all of them.

I was pondering over whether to tell them the truth or not, but I decided to hang onto the information for a while longer. Sometimes, when you tell people they have a ghost or a spirit it can change their lives quite drastically. Some people choose to move out of their home, sell their property, or stay in it as little as possible. If only people would understand a home belongs to the person whose name is on the rent book, or on the mortgage contract. It's the ghost that needs to move out!

I needed to be responsive and responsible to the 'dead' and the 'living' so I started with the spirit lady. Plonking myself on a chair I blocked out the women and focused on the spirit who told me her husband had spent a long time in hospital. She was married to him for most of her life. He had been sent home to die as nothing more could be done for him. She told me how she would run the taps to fill a bowl of water to wash him and keep him clean. She explained how she would get up in the night to check on him, just to make sure he was still breathing. I guess that's what people do when they know someone has limited time. Only he had gone but she still carried on as if he were still here. She hadn't found the white light for some reason.

I continued moving from room to room and couldn't help but feel a sense of sadness. The four ladies being curious asked if I had picked up anything. They thought I was behaving a little strange. Nothing new there! I guess they found me strange because I wasn't talking to them. I was using my mind to talk to someone they could not see. I decided I could tell them who I was talking to if I put it in a delicate way. I knew this spirit needed to be rescued from her torment, so I helped her to step into the white light that opened its door to receive her where she took a step and crossed over into the spirit world.

I explained to the housemates the presence of the lovely elderly lady. I smiled as I explained how she was the wife of a man to whom she had been married to for most of her life. She had been confused in thinking he was coming back and would fill bowls of water to wash him down. She couldn't accept he had gone and so carried on with her caring duties, she didn't know where to else to go. She hadn't found the white light. They all smiled and gave a sigh of relief. I gave a sigh of relief as I knew I had accomplished explaining the spirit lady as 'someone's wife', and not as a 'ghost' haunting the house!

A few days later when I bumped into Gemma she told me things had completely stopped, much to her surprise. Much to my own surprise! The housemates were all happy to sleep where they should be ... in their own bed in their own room! The feeling of my first spiritual release, and completion of a successful crossing over of a spirit, for me, was euphoric in many ways. It gave me confidence that I could do the work for and on behalf of spirit. It made me feel confident knowing that people who ask for my help will get my help.

Locations investigated also include: H. M Royal Navy, Plymouth, Syon Park House, Isleworth, The Crown, Amersham, The Sun, Hertford, Avoncroft Museum, Bristol, Inveraray Jail, Inveraray, Reels Cinema, Plymouth, The Ostrich Inn, Colnbrook

Spirit Behaving Badly

Another investigation took me out to an elderly gentleman, Mr Malone, who resided at a warden's home. Mr Malone was clearly embarrassed at calling me out and didn't mind telling me. I knew only too well how difficult it was for him to ask me to be there. He had always been a true sceptic of ghosts but was now beside himself. He claimed he was seeing visions of ghosts at the bottom of his bed when he slept. Night after night he would be woken up by more than one ghostly person pulling at his feet. Often he would be pulled out of bed.

He grew increasingly concerned of the visitations because the lady who lived in the flat before him also had visitations. She also experienced the same. The poor lady had, wrongly or rightly, been moved into a home where she would get 24/7 care. There was nothing wrong with her mind. Others thought different.

The poor man sat nervously talking me through the mysterious things that were now making his life difficult. These things he described were scaring him witless. He didn't want to live with this experience, or the ghosts. I sympathised with him over a cup of tea as I listened carefully to what he was attempting to explain. He had made me a nice cup of tea in a bone china cup that came complete with a saucer. Drinking tea out of a cup and saucer was a bit fancy for me. It did bring a smile to my face though as I remembered how my grandmother would get out her best crockery when she had guests.

I finished the tea in no time; I was a bit nervous holding both a cup and saucer together at the same time, I needed to dispose of them quickly. Visions of broken china scattered all over the floor came to mind. Standing up I placed them safely on the nearest table. Guiding me to the room with the view, the bedroom, Mr Malone anxiously spoke of his alarm clock. Every morning at 3:00am it would go off for no apparent reason. The alarm was never switched on. It was safe to note that the clock had taken up time in his bedside cabinet, out of sight. I walked over to the corner of the room and sat in a chair talking to myself in my mind as I do. Well, talking to spirit actually but I couldn't let Mr Malone see me do this. We'd have both been questioning our sanity! I wasn't sitting there for too long, thank goodness, when I felt the energy of spirit come close. The spirit wasn't speaking to me but I was speaking to him. I told him I was there because of him and how naughty he had been behaving. I told him his behaviour was not acceptable and he had to move on, there was no need for him to be there any longer. In return I was greeted with silence. This spirit man wasn't answering me.

The spirit was going to be hard work but it didn't bother me, I could stay there and nag him into another death or he could leave. I returned back to the living room where Mr Malone was sitting at his computer. He had been waiting patiently for news of my findings, only I couldn't give anything. I was still in conversation with the spirit, albeit it was a one-way dialogue.

Before I could sit down Mr Malone spoke of his happiness and love for his grand-children. He was eager to show me photos his daughter had emailed earlier in the day. I watched him as he downloaded the file of photos and attempted to print one off. The photos didn't print, but to our amazement a print out of a drawing with a big house did. Spread right across the centre of the page was the word *"H.E.L.P"*. He was dumbfounded as he told me he had never seen that before. I hadn't either but I had experienced the phenomenon before when "THIS IS US AND WE ARE HERE" appeared on my computer screen, not once but twice.

I had no explanation to offer the poor man, not that I would want to anyway, he was anxious enough. I sat back in the chair and communicated with the male spirit I had spoken to earlier. I had felt his presence for some time and felt sure that somehow he was to blame for the printing. Again, I asked him to cross over into the white light and leave the home as it was no longer his. I told him he was frightening the resident and he wouldn't like it done to him. I conversed with the spirit man a little longer when he finally decided to talk to me. He gave me some information but the gentleman could not relate to it. Or perhaps the gentleman could not remember. It didn't matter though, I was happy to watch the spirit step into the white light. My job was done.

I received an email a few weeks later to thank me for the work I had done, as he put it, 'He can sleep better now', and his clock doesn't bother him anymore. More importantly, he doesn't have to fight off *'spirit behaving badly'*. Furthermore, he isn't going to be put into a 'home'. Guess my visit was well timed!

Things that go Bump in the Night

Sometimes I wonder who is more disturbed, the 'living' or the 'dead'. It doesn't really matter though does it; since there is no 'dead', well, not really. That's what Sandra thought too when she called me to tell me her property was 'haunted.' She believed the 'dead' was haunting her. Her partner Keith also believed in the 'dead' and seemed to think his flat was going through unexplained changes. These changes were caused by ghosts who would move things around.

Apparently, when Sandra stayed at the flat with Keith overnight they couldn't get a wink of sleep. Both suffered a tremendous fear as they relayed to me *'things that go bump in the night'* when the lights went out. There were things that were falling off shelves and moving from the place in which they should have been. They convinced themselves they were haunted. They were sure they were being visited by the 'dead'.

The hauntings were taking place in both of their properties and I wanted to know why. Suffice to say, I didn't get a totally good feeling at all from these total strangers, I was sure there was more to it than I had been told.

I made a date with Keith and arrived at his small flat. Sandra greeted me at the door and directed me to the bedroom that was the cause of the nightly activity. The room was quite dark given its small size. I sunk myself down onto the rather low bed as I listened to Sandra and Keith talk me through the events that had been occurring.

Their biggest problem appeared to be the objects on the shelves falling off of their own accord, especially during the night. My observation of the shelves, positioned half way up the walls was to note how over cramped with objects they were. The possibility of something falling off could be a reasonable explanation. I was prepared to accept this theory until I felt a coldness appear in front of me. A sign that spirit was close by.

Sitting down on the edge of the bed I told the spirit why I was there. I told the spirit not to be afraid and that I was there to help. I could feel the energy to be male and wanted to encourage him to use more energy; I wanted to see him clearly. I kept talking to him, I told him who I was, why I was there and what I was doing. It didn't take too long before I saw him materialise in front of me. A bowling ball was tucked underneath his arm. He gave me his name and I passed the information and his description onto the couple. Looking at me with surprise they knew straight away who it was. They were pleased their friend had come to visit them and could perhaps now have a restful night's sleep. I thanked the spirit for coming forward, working with me and guided him into the divine white light.

I was to meet Sandra and Keith again just a week later. Sandra called me to tell me 'things' were happening at her property too. She was desperate for me to visit her, especially as she couldn't sleep at night when she was alone. Even when Keith stayed overnight none of them could relax. Their sleep was once again being disturbed by things falling off shelves, objects moving of their own accord. Once again they were experiencing *'things that go bump in the night'*. I still felt there was more to these two people than met the eye, however, I agreed to visit her flat.

I arrived at Sandra's flat telling myself I wouldn't be there long. It had been a long day and a busy week for me. I just wanted to do the work, if there was any to be done then go home. I could tell they were pleased to see me when they opened the front door. I remember thinking how unlucky they were to be haunted in two very different locations. Sandra took my arm and led me through to the sitting room. She stood up whilst I sat on the sofa. I listened intently as she described accounts of what was happening in the middle of the night. Things were still being moved around and falling off shelves. There was also the feeling of someone, or something pressing down on her bed whilst she slept.

I went through my nice little ritual of asking spirit to come forward and speak to me. My request was adhered to as an energy gathered round my feet. As the energy became stronger I heard my spirit guide, Hannah, whisper a name, it was an unusual name and felt it belonged to an animal rather than a human being. I relayed the information to Sandra and she told me it was the name of her kitten, I blessed the kitten. It's always comforting to know that our pets in the spirit world are close by us.

I was ready to stand up and leave thinking I'd finished, as you do, when a spirit lady came and sat next to me. She had such a lovely gentleness about her I just had to find out who she was. I'm not one for refusing a spirit or two so I let her speak. With her walking frame in front of her, she seemed to be excited about not needing it any longer. Nevertheless, she didn't want to let it go. She gave me her name and a man's name which I passed onto Sandra and who confirmed the lady had once lived in her flat. The man whose name had been given still lived next door and hadn't been well. I told Sandra she had come because she was keeping an eye on her neighbour, she was also giving him spiritual healing. The spirit lady told me they had been neighbours for many years; it was the least she could do for all the help he had given her during her earthly years. I thought this was very kind of her and such a noble thing to do.

I couldn't figure out why Sandra and Keith attracted spirits to them, so I asked Hannah, my spirit guide what was going on. She told me Sandra was into the paranormal and dabbled a bit, well, quite a bit actually. I asked Sandra to confirm if she was interested in the paranormal and the 'dead.' Of course, she acknowledged she was and claimed to be a 'medium' but didn't know much about what a 'medium' does, much to my annoyance.

Far be it for me to tell people who they think they are, I advised her to learn how to work with spirit by going to Spiritualist church. Attracting spirit into your home can be quite easy for some, but enticing them to leave can be very much harder. I decided I wouldn't help her if she called again as she needed to take some responsibility for herself.

It was no surprise to get a call a few weeks later from Sandra to tell me her car was haunted because it kept breaking down. She asked me if I could call round and sit in the car to find out what was wrong with it. I asked Hannah, my spirit guide what could possibly be wrong this time. My very thought was confirmed when Hannah told me the car wasn't haunted it was merely dying of 'old age'.

Bless Sandra; she was somewhat surprised when I declined her invitation to visit. I delicately told her, 'Cars age and need replacement body parts, it would be better if a mechanic sat in your car rather than a medium.' Whilst she tended to agree, I didn't feel she was convinced with my theory. My theory being that it was nothing to do with spirit. The old car was laid to rest when Sandra purchased a new one.

Haunted Mirror

From the outside, the hotel didn't look all that big but inside it was very spacious. With its elegance and maturity I could really feel the atmosphere as I blended with its energies and ambience of times gone by. The Sun Hotel, Hitchin, Hertfordshire is a traditional old English 1500's Coaching Inn. It was once headquarters to over three thousand parliamentary soldiers quartered in the town. Hitchin Justices, the Council of War and government officials were just some of the posh gentile folk who would use the hotel to conduct their business.

My business was to find out if the place was haunted and I had taken my team with me to find out. The hotel manager would also be joining us for the night and I was glad he did, he proved to be an important witness later on in the evening. I could tell the manager, his staff and my team were all going to get along very well. We blended nicely with one another as we commenced a tour of the hotel.

I was glad we started the tour on the ground floor; it gave me an opportunity to venture outside and to view the back of the building. Stepping out into the courtyard I felt the snow as it fell gently from the sky, dusting the ground as it began to settle. The building looked quite quaint and picturesque as the snow covered the roof tops. I stayed long enough just to embrace the softness of the snow before returning back inside. My team were already unpacking equipment and knew exactly what they needed to do. Their professionalism and dedication always amazed me. We worked well together.

We began our baseline (preliminary) testing of the rooms we were to hold vigils in at 7:00pm. These tests would consist of temperature and EMF readings. The mediums, including myself, would test psychic energies in the areas we had been allocated to investigate. This allowed our senses to get a feel of which areas would be spiritually active. The area we chose to work from was the small bar area adjacent to the ballroom. This proved to be a good choice, as we were later to discover.

Some of the locations we were offered to investigate would not have proved at all suitable because of the music blasting out from an adjoining hall. It didn't matter though because we avoided areas in close proximity of the music and instead investigated one bedroom, the ballroom and small bar area. It's never quantity that matters but always quality!

The ballroom was the largest of the rooms we examined and the one which gave us our best piece of photographic evidence. The room itself was dark and empty with a high ceiling and wooden flooring. Footsteps echoed as I paced the floorboards from one end of the hall to the other. It was quiet an eerie feeling and I did feel a little haunted when I heard someone call my name 'Goldy' and no one was there. But it was the curtains that got my 'normal' girlie attention. What I would have given for those long heavy curtains which draped so stylishly and proudly over the long paned windows. I was in complete awe of this room.

An ornate mirror hung high and haunted on one of the walls; it bothered me, I knew it was haunted and would later find out exactly why. I have a thing about mirrors so I tried not to look at it. Instead I positioned myself in the middle of the ballroom ready to feel the energies that surrounded me. Standing still in the quietness of the night I felt myself going back in time as I danced to the music and ambience of an orchestra. I could have quite happily glided around the room wearing my make-believe ball gown. But, there was work to be done and my team were waiting in the bar.

In an area adjacent to the ballroom was a small bar scattered with a few tables and an over-crowding of chairs. The tables and chairs were re-arranged so could we set up the combi (TV and video recorder) close to the ballroom door. With a spy camera and length of cabling attached to the combi it was positioned in the ballroom to record activity directly back to the TV. Once we were happy everything had been set up to record we headed up to the bedroom.

The team held a very successful vigil in bedroom 21 where we witnessed the audible sounds of a clock ticking. Strangely enough there was no clock with such a mechanism in the room. I was pleased that the manager of the hotel took part in the vigil and was present in the room to hear this phenomenon. He was able to confirm a man once connected to the hotel would walk the length and breadth of the corridors, winding up clocks that hung on the walls. Without spending any further time in the room we headed back to the small bar adjacent to the ballroom. We set up a few empty cassette cases on paper and drew lines round the case carefully so as not to move it out of place. We also used some coins placed on paper to draw round and position on tables. If spirit were here their function would have been to move the objects out of position. With a bar in the proximity it would have been a good time to have had a few drinks, but I'm not one to mix my spirits!

The team were busy setting up trigger objects around the bar area as I stood watching the TV monitor. The video was still running and recording the empty ballroom. Whilst watching the screen I saw the figure of a woman appear in one of the mirrors in the ballroom. It was the very mirror that had bothered me earlier. Fortunately for me, one of the voice recorders picked up my voice indicating this sighting, an observation which proved to be a good piece of psychic evidence on my part. I had a feeling there was something dodgy about that mirror! I didn't hesitate to grab my camera, hurry into the room and snap away at the mirror taking photographs.

It was one of the photographs that later proved to be a key piece of evidence we had collected during the course of this investigation. A woman had been captured in the mirror I didn't like. I couldn't argue with what I saw, the evidence was apparent. And, further proof in that I had verbally indicated my vision of the woman on the recording. But, what was significantly strange about this image was that the figure was not a mirror image reflection. The angle of the image made it exceptionally interesting because the woman in the mirror was positioned at a sideways angle. I decided it was time to get to the know spirit better, and time for a séance to see if we could draw spirit closer.

I like to form a rapport with spirit by informing them why we are there, why we do what we do and ask for their help. Sometimes we get it, sometimes we don't. However, I asked for spirit's help and we got it during our last séance when something quite unusual happened. I had asked spirit to touch one of the team as proof of their presence, and of their survival. I don't think any of us could have anticipated as to what would happen to one of our team members. And, to be honest, spirit couldn't have given proof to a more sceptic person if they tried.

The team sceptic felt his wrists itching and burning throughout the séance, not that it overly concerned him at the time. But once the séance was over he expressed concerns about an area of his chest. As he lifted up his jumper there were red new scratch marks that looked like someone had run their nails across his chest. Scratch marks also appeared over his wrists positioned on top of a Chinese tattoo, which when interpreted meant 'LIFE.' One can only conclude that spirit were giving us the evidence we had asked for and that there is *life* after death. Thanks were given to spirit for the validation of their existence in the afterlife.

Haunted Séance

Inveraray, Scotland, March 20th 2005. My eleventh wedding anniversary and I would be a bit of a long way from London. I could enjoy investigating Inveraray Jail and celebrating my wedding anniversary at the same time. I couldn't forget something as important as my wedding anniversary now could I? Oops, perhaps I could!

I'd always wanted to visit Scotland, so when a colleague of mine, Mitch, mentioned investigating the jail I thought it seemed like too good an opportunity to resist. Of course, having to travel almost six hundred miles I needed to check with Hubby. Not because he would be the driver, but because of my medical condition. None of us was sure if I would be able to eat sufficiently due to my condition and my allergy to diary and wheat.

After giving it a lot of thought, we both agreed to make the journey having organised with a bed & breakfast hotel my dietary requirements. Or, at least I thought it was organised. Still, I knew Hubby would drive me straight home should I need to leave. I did, and he did.

Nothing is ever straight forward, well, not in my life anyway. I had one more mission to accomplish and that was to get the jail to agree. I contacted the manager who was very pleasant and agreed to the visit. All I needed next was to calm my nerves for the journey. I'm not the best traveller, unless, of course, I can get the traffic to move over from whatever lane we happen to be travelling in at the time.

All packed up and ready to go, we headed off. Most normal people would enjoy the scenic views that we passed *en route* to Scotland, but not me. I didn't like the journey, there were too many mountains for my liking and I'm not an admirer of heights; but I couldn't move the mountains, now could I! After a night's stop over at Mitch's house we continued the journey and arrived safely at Inveraray and our Bed and Breakfast. The hotel had been converted from an old church which was most intriguing, or convenient!

I was almost tempted to investigate the hotel, but had to get to the jail to meet the staff for our pre-planned, pre-site survey. It was only a short distance to the jail and Mitch, a Medium herself accompanied me. The jail, built in 1820 was to keep men, women and children in the confines of its prisons, courtyard and exercise yards. The sentence for a petty theft would see the criminal branded with a hot iron, or had their ear nailed to a post. Some criminals were publicly whipped.

The jailer himself met us in the gift shop and led us round our first building, the 'Women's Prison'. I couldn't begin to imagine how it must have felt for women to be locked up in such a confined and cold space, let alone the children. The building had a feeling of despair and hopelessness. I couldn't help but feel sadness and pain for the women condemned to the prison, especially those who were pregnant.

We made our way to the 'Wash House' whereupon entering the building I had a vision of a woman lying on the floor. My vision showed me that the woman was unconscious with blood coming from a gaping head wound. When I turned away I saw a vision of two men running away from the scene. I mentioned what I had seen to the jailer who explained that male prisoners often acted as protectors for the women. Women were notably famous for their in-house fighting.

The next area we visited was the 'Courthouse' which had its own air of intimidation. Mannequins dressed in historic costumes of their era looked life size and realistic in the replicated courtroom. It made me feel uncomfortable sitting amongst the mannequins. It felt like time had stood hauntingly still.

A few short steps out of the courtroom took us across the yard to the 'Men's Prison' into cells that were filled with heavy residue energies. Within this building was a cell known as the 'Whipping Cell', used for the very function its name holds. Besides its name, the sheer purpose of what went on held a nauseating feeling. I was certainly not looking forward to the evening's investigation in this cell, but I'd seen enough, it was time to leave and I was hungry.

I hadn't managed to eat anything since arriving, but then I knew how difficult it would be to find a suitable place. The kitchen at the hotel was locked up so my plans to use the microwave were scuppered. However, being psychic I had packed a few items of my own that I could merrily tuck into. Just as well I had packed something because I needed energy, lack of food made me tired.

I thought of having a half hour sleep on the bed and meet all the team later. But, with so many people coming in and out of my room sleep was something that would have to wait. At 6.45pm it was a little early to go start the investigation, but as no one would settle I decided to round my team up and head to the jail.

I could feel the excitement and energies coming from members of the team as we knocked on the large heavy doors of the jail. There was an eeriness as the door slowly opened and our jailer was standing on the other side. We were shown to our meeting base for the night in the kitchen, a good place for refreshments, of which the team had plenty.

After a quick walk round the jail we planned the vigils in order of preference. As with any vigil, mediums advise on where commence first. Unless you're me, in which case I always leave the best till last. However, I couldn't wait to get started and set up our first vigil in the courtroom. It was here Mitch connected with a small crying child; he was nine years old and gave his name as 'Jamie'. His sentence was for thieving. Mitch spoke to him telling him that his mother was waiting for him. His mother had come to collect him from the other side and both were helped to cross over into the white light.

From the courtroom we made our way to the 'Men's Prison' where we set up trigger objects and motion detectors, (Motion detectors are used to trigger an alarm when activated). One of my trigger objects was a small heart shaped sponge on a blackboard and sieved over with flour. If the sponge moved out of place it would be noticeable. I placed it in the 'Gaelic Cell' where three lifelike mannequins were positioned on the floor replicating a game of cards. These mannequins spooked me more than those in the courtroom. I felt more frightened of them than of spirit, but it wasn't spirit that frightened me. There was definitely a high charge of energies in this cell that caused one member of my team to feel nauseous. I had to stop him setting up the trigger objects and instructed him to leave the cell.

The trigger objects didn't disappoint us either. I returned to the cell with another team member some time later to check the sponge we had set up earlier. On observation we found it had moved by maybe a quarter of an inch. I know the cell had been locked off (out of bounds) so it would not have been possible for any team member to re-enter.

The next cell the 'Whipping Cell' I wasn't particularly looking forward to since visiting it earlier in the day. The psychic energies were extremely strong and I sensed colossal fear and pain. I wasn't going to let my feelings get the better of me so took a deep breath before entering. I have never refused to enter any room in any location I have investigated and I wasn't going to start now. In the centre of the cell was a wooden table with leather straps attached. The straps were for the purpose of holding the prisoner down during punishment. I touched the table but removed my hands very quickly, I didn't like the feeling I connected to. I didn't stay there long.

Crossing the corridor to conduct a vigil in an adjacent cell, and with the whole team present we closed the cell door. In the darkness of the night I proceeded to ask for confirmation of spirit presence but was overcome with feelings of nausea. The cell door had to be opened to allow air to flow in so I could breathe and overcome the feeling. We were ready to move on.

Squeezing quite nicely in our next cell we all sat on the concrete floor. I recited my normal ritual of why we were there as I asked for spirit to communicate with us. We sat for several minutes in silence when suddenly there was a loud shouting noise coming from the cell next door. The technical team had set up an EVP, (electronic voice phenomena) recorder in there earlier, so we went in and checked to see if it had recorded anything. When the recorder was played back it had picked up a loud angry voice shouting 'Get Out.' I suppose that was a good a cue as any to leave and head for the old kitchen to do a séance.

A glass was set up on the kitchen table and two pieces of paper with the words 'Yes', and 'No' set either side.' Four mediums took their seats round the table offering prayers and psychic protection to those who took part in the séance. Using Spirit of the Glass or conducting a séance is definitely something I would not recommend at home. If you have no experience of working with the 'dead', don't work with the 'dead', because they will want to work with you!

We established contact with a spirit who moved the glass in answer to our questions. The spirit was a female called Anne (with an E, she stressed), and who had contacted Mitch before the jail visit. Spirit often make contact with a medium before we get to a location so this was not unusual.

Further communications with the woman through the use of 'Spirit of the Glass' and psychic communication revealed she was in an agitated state. She said she had been accused of killing her new born baby but vehemently denied this. She continued to explain that, 'The baby was born dead,' and she wanted to, 'Set the record straight.' I told her she had achieved that by communicating with us. We all thanked her for the information she gave and crossed her into the light. I believe her spirit to now be at peace.

It was 22:30pm when the team gathered in Cell 9 and we all sat squashed together once again on the cold concrete floor. Sitting in complete silence we heard a motion detector trigger from the cell below us. As the alarm sounded members of the team noticed a strong smell. The odour of stale alcohol and leather filled the cell we sat in. Strange things were going on.

Things went from good to very good as we held a vigil in cell 10. But for one member of the team this cell would be a little disturbing. In the centre of the cell we had placed a chalkboard on the floor which he appeared to be angry about for no apparent reason. I remember he was so angry he wanted to kick it. This would have been very much out of character for him and assumed his energies had blended with other negative energies that were present.

As the night went on many more strange things occurred that could not be explained, especially with the voice recorders. There were many voices recorded on our equipment that could not be explained. Especially the voices in the 'Wardens' room where two people appeared to be laughing and joking, yet this room was locked off so no one could enter. The voices were not recognised as belonging to any of my team.

All team members are instructed to double check gadgets before leaving them in locked off areas. So, when a motion detector in cell 12 became activated and sounded an alarm two of the team went to check. However, on inspection it was noticed the device had not actually been switched on. It was time for another séance.

At 02:45am we conducted our last séance in the staff room using the 'Spirit of the Glass.' I said earlier not to try this form of communication at home because it is not a game and can cause many problems. Spirits can be both negative and positive energies, so unless you are trained in controlling spirit, crossing them over and closing down a séance you may find they stay.

Sitting at the table were three mediums that performed the séance, each medium asked questions and spirit used the glass once again to respond to 'yes' or 'no' questions. The 'Spirit of the Glass' was working well when asked questions posed by the mediums, but not for anyone else. When four members of the team who were not mediums took to the table it had a different effect. The glass would not move despite several attempts to get spirit to respond and work with us. Since we were not getting any movement with the glass or response from spirit, we closed the séance and left the table.

I hadn't anticipated what would happen in 'Cell 10' when we held a vigil there. I was to experience a heavy energy force that gave me a thumping headache and another member complained of feeling dizzy. We didn't spend too much time in this location since some of the team members experienced feelings of nausea. Those who felt nauseous had to leave and physically started vomiting.

After ten hours spent at the jail it was time to end the investigation. It had been a long and interesting evening with both the physical (living) and the non-physical (dead). Our mission was accomplished as we were able to collect an assortment of solid evidence. The evidence consisted of a photograph showing the image of a lady outside the window of a second floor building. Food was smelt inside and outside one of the buildings. In addition, various voice phenomena were picked up on tape recordings, a trigger object had moved out of place and a motion detector could not be explained.

As we headed back to our hotel I was pleased in thinking we had got what we came for, evidence. It had been an incredibly long day and long night with the travelling and the investigation, now I was tired. I was cold, tired and hungry as I fell into bed totally exhausted relaying the night's events to Hubby who had stayed in rather than join us. He didn't like investigating so never came along. But, I couldn't sleep and couldn't wait for breakfast. I had less than two hours to wait before I could have a slap up meal of eggs on toast.

I thought Hubby and I would be the first ones down to the dining room but was pleasantly surprised to find some of my team already there. It was an even bigger surprise as they all shouted, 'Happy anniversary.' I wanted the floor to open up underneath me as I realised I had forgotten our anniversary. My Hubby rubbed my nose it in and wished me 'Happy anniversary' too as I sat mortified wondering how I had managed to forget. I was very embarrassed since I had deliberately planned the weekend away to coincide with our anniversary. Did he forgive me? What do you think?

As if that wasn't bad enough, Hubby had to drive me home earlier than planned because it was impossible for me to eat; this made my medical condition worse. I felt disappointed in that I hadn't finished everything I wanted to do. I wanted another walk round the jail, I also needed feeding!

Haunted Footsteps

Investigating a magnificent stately house in London, which for privacy reasons cannot be named, not once, but four times as part of an on-going project was a dream come true. Its past and current occupants span back many generations. To this day the house remains home to the ghost of a very famous lady. The stately home with a wealth of history behind it was residence to many Royals of the English throne. Having visited the property many times, I can tell you between day time and night time the appearance and transformation of its look and feel was very noticeable. This magnificent property posed many challenges, least that of fear itself.

My first challenge to clinch an investigation was to present my port-folio, which I would base on my experience and knowledge as a paranormal research investigator. Presenting my work would not be a problem as I always believe it to be one of excellence. I had done a great deal of researching the paranormal and getting to know my subject field, so I drew comfort in knowing what I was talking about. There was nothing that would excite me more than talking to others about my accomplishments. Of course, I couldn't have learnt what it is that I know today if it weren't for those gave me the opportunity, and to whom I sincerely thank.

Opportunities always came by chance and I always seemed to have a knack of contacting people at the right time. My timing was well received when I contacted the stately home. Apparently, people of good standing had been witness to unexplained phenomena as well as ghostly apparitions. There was no question they were in need of a visit, if not an investigation.

I had been offered an opportunity to meet with the estate manager of this world famous house and I was going to take it. I had no hesitation in arranging a half day's holiday from work, I always booked time off if I needed to go somewhere of particular paranormal interest.

Leaving my home, I had my port-folio tucked safely in my briefcase. Butterflies were spinning round in my stomach as Hubby drove me to the stately house. We parked at the end of the long gravel drive that led up to the house. Getting out of the car I realised my mistake had been to wear stiletto shoes. I would wobble and not walk as I stepped across the stones making my way up to the back door. I left Hubby sitting in the car.

My stomach was churning over with nerves as I made it to the back door. I was expecting to see a large door knocker, or an antique door handle that you had to pull, but instead found a small push button bell on the door frame. I pushed the button and waited before a lovely lady pulled the door open. She was wearing a big smile as she greeted me and invited me in. We walked along the dark long corridors which seemed to go on forever as we made our way to the estate manager's office. I felt nervous, but wasn't sure if it was because of the meeting or because of the building, I decided it was both. However, I wasn't going to let my nerves get the better of me as I was introduced to the manager and other members of his staff.

I was in complete awe of the antique décor and exceptionally large portraits that hung on the walls. I thought they wouldn't be any use in my house; I wouldn't have a wall large enough to accommodate one! This house was certainly alive with spirit; I was praying they would not interfere with my meeting. Sitting down, I presented and demonstrated my work as a paranormal research investigator. The manager and staff who sat round the big wooden table with me were just as excited as I was. It took just over an hour for me to finish showing off my port folio and could see from the expressions on their faces they were pleased. I was pleased as I let out a big sigh of relief. It wasn't as bad as I had anticipated. I hadn't packed my things away before I was invited to tour round the house. I had expected having to return for a tour round at a later date.

Walking round the house with members of staff I realised we were not alone; a spirit was walking with us. I wanted to tell the spirit, 'Not now luvvie I'm busy', but felt it would be mean so I allowed him to chat. It was a little difficult trying to hold a conversation with both the 'living' and the 'dead', and not exactly easy to do without being noticed by my hosts.

I apologised and explained to Becky and Dexter, the two members of staff that a spirit was with me and wanted to make contact with one of them. It was not something they had expected but were only too pleased for me to give them any information I could. Dexter knew straight away who the spirit was and nervously identified him to be his deceased father. I say 'nervously' because he never expected his dad to come through, neither did I! I cannot disclose the information that followed as it was private and meant for the recipient only. From the look on Dexter's face I could see he was pleased, it had made his day. His dad wasn't the only one who wanted to make contact; I could feel a queue of spirits begin to form alongside me but knew I had to leave. I knew Hubby had been waiting long enough in the car and I could feel his energies reaching out to me!

Shaking hands and thanking everyone for their hospitality, I wobbled back up the gravel drive to the car. I had fallen in love with the house, not that I could live there as it was too ominous. Nonetheless, I couldn't contain my excitement as I tried to relay to Hubby details of the meeting and the events that followed. I hadn't finished getting the first words out before he interrupted me and told of his experience with the car radio. Apparently, he had tried to listen to at least one radio station but found the channel kept changing and he had to turn it off. It was obvious someone from the spirit world had been keeping him company whilst I was away.

My presentation proved to be successful because I was granted permission to take my team and investigate in July 2005. The months leading up to the investigation dragged. All I wanted to do was get in there and get to work. I had my team organised and knew they were just as excited as I was, but I never told them the name of the venue. I could only tell them on the night, especially my two seasoned mediums that had been long standing members of the team. I didn't want any information given to them to be contaminated; neither could I myself use any information which would appear contaminated. As the organiser, it kind of took the shine off using my psychic and mediumistic skills. I would mostly have to rely on audio and visual evidence as well as information given by the mediums.

I was glad when the night of the investigation arrived. I couldn't contain my excitement any longer when my team of twelve investigators arrived at my house. Unable to hold onto my excitement I blurted out where we were going. They all grinned, I was glad they were just as excited as I was as it charged the energies between us. Not that we needed charging.

Everyone helped to check the functionality of equipment and insert new batteries and tapes into the gadgets that required these products. Kitting up battery operated equipment is something that is done either before we get to a venue or on arrival. It assures everyone the consumables are new and have not been used before. Besides, drainage in batteries is quite a common phenomenon on investigations and hard to explain when sudden drainage occurs.

After we had loaded everything into the cars we set off for a night of the 'unknown.' Exciting isn't it, not knowing what to expect, if anything at all? The cars drove up the long gravel driveway which felt like *déjà vu* for me, minus the heels! Becky and Dexter were waiting there to greet us and I made the introductions. Everyone was grinning from ear to ear and looking forward to the night ahead.

Heading for the kitchen, our base for the night, we decided and collaborated on our plan of action. Our first plan of action was to conduct some base line testing. This meant some of us would have to walk round the house.

As there were three mediums present, including myself, we decided to walk round together with team members assigned to accompany each of us. Their task would be to take notes of anything the mediums picked up on. We were careful not to allow one another to hear what we reported to avoid contamination.

Walking down the long corridors was unnerving, even with the lights on! It gave me an adrenalin rush and a feeling of paranormal excitement. The feeling you get when you don't know what to expect. I wanted to know more about this house. I wanted to know why the owner, who rarely visited, and its staff had been troubled by different types of phenomena. Sightings of ghostly figures were not uncommon in this house.

Making our way back to base and the kitchen I hadn't got a clue as to which room to concentrate on first. Deciding which location you start and end up in is something that cannot be pre-planned. It would be normal to go with the flow of spirit and where they lead you, or as in my case, my spirit guides advice.

Hannah always left the best room till last. I used to find this odd; it would be hours into the night before we could start on the best and by then we would all be bloody knackered! I trusted her and always did as she told me, so saved the best till last. What's the point in having someone give you guidance if you didn't use it!

Back in the kitchen and our base for the night the team sorted out all the equipment. Some members of the team made a decision as to where to set up audio and visual equipment, other team members made a decision as to where to set up trigger objects. Many members of my team have a few years experience of investigating the paranormal, so no training was required.

Some of the equipment was taken to rooms that would be locked off and out of bounds for a period of time during the investigation. Once the rooms were locked off a glow-stick would be placed outside the door. The glow-sticks were to remind each of us there was an experiment being conducted in that area. All areas that were locked off were checked for health and safety issues. Looking after your team members is paramount in comparison to the sighting of a ghost. (Insuring an event is also advisable especially against damages to tangible goods within the property).

I split the team into two groups, with one medium and Dexter in one team and the other medium and Becky in my team. My team headed for the long gallery, the darkest, coldest and spookiest of places in the whole house. The other team ventured down to the bottom part of the house. As I was organising tasks and equipment, I couldn't help feeling I was being followed by people other than those of my team.

The next event proved to be unbelievable, unexplainable and a little nerve-jangling. I'm not one to get scared easily, if I say so myself. If I do feel uncomfortable I know I can handle myself but this next event was intriguing. The team were just entering the gallery which was very dark and had no lighting, except for our torches. Suddenly we encountered out of nowhere an almighty loud rattling noise. Wanting to run off but thinking better of it I took the team and walked down the gallery towards the far end. It was here we witnessed the doors shaking quite violently then stop. When we opened the doors we expected to see someone from the other team standing there. I thought perhaps someone was either lost or had come to find us for a very good reason. I never allow team members to wander off on their own willy nilly. When we opened the doors, there was no-one there!

We set up a monitor and squatted on the carpet which stretched wall to wall; thank goodness there were no cold floors, but it was exceptionally freezing cold. I have a strange habit of working with energy from the floor upwards, so squatting down anywhere didn't really bother me. An eerie silence filled the whole room.

I checked the team to make sure everyone was ok; I always worry about people and how they may feel or react. It was whilst I was looking behind a member of the team that my eyes followed what looked like the black shape of a cat, or perhaps a rat. The mysterious shape ran from one side of the room to the other. It was unlikely to appear again so I didn't think any more of it. Well, not really.

Temperatures in the gallery kept fluctuating, mostly getting colder. Strange really because once you're in a room your body should perhaps adjust to the room temperature. This room however was very serene, it felt like we shouldn't talk or move. After the episode with the doors rattling I wanted to move ...out! The second time we heard doors rattling was for a good reason, the other team had decided to join us. We relayed what had happened with the doors and were told it wasn't them. Dexter also confirmed it wasn't anyone from his team, but they had heard it on the floor below as they were leaving to go to their own area. They thought it was us!

Our next task was to hold a séance. How I love a good old séance, especially when 'Spirit of the Glass' is used. We found a large round table, gathered some chairs and laid out the Lexicon cards. Placing the glass in the middle of the table with 'yes', 'no' papers written either side of it we started to communicate with the deceased. I should reiterate that it is unwise to use this method to communicate with spirit if you are not trained. Opening and closing a séance in a correct way is extremely important. People who are inexperienced and have used this form of communication often find the spirits who make contact stay. Some spirits have been known to be very mischievous, not the sort of entity you would want hanging around your home. Trust me.

The first spirit person to use the glass as their channel came through to connect to one of the staff at the house. As the glass moved from letter to letter it spelt out a name. The name was connected to Dexter seated at the table, his father had made contact with us again. It was quite a surprise and an emotional moment for all of us; a surprise that the spirit had stayed since my first visit and since his first contact with me. He proved that although he was on the other side, he was still very much around his son. Dexter was totally overwhelmed by what he had witnessed.

We took a break to allow the energies to calm before returning back to the table, and another séance. The next deceased person who came through gave his name and the type of work he did at the house. Whilst the information could not be validated at the time, it was confirmed a few days later by a member of staff. It was most probable that he was a contractor because the name and other information appeared to be true. But, spending the night sitting round a séance table didn't get work done. The séance was closed, spirit thanked and we moved on.

There were so many rooms in this house to be nosey in it was like an 'Aladdin's Cave.' Rooms filled with artefacts and memorabilia of times gone by. In comparison with today, I wondered how people got by without the use of electrical gadgets, especially with the absence of a vacuum cleaner. I felt rather sorry for the servants who would have had to keep this stately home clean, it wasn't small. There would have been many servants running from floor to floor to wait on the 'Master' of the house. At the sound of a bell, footsteps would be running the never ending length of the corridors. Maids and servants panic stricken in case they were late reaching a room. It left me knackered just thinking about it, too much exercise for my liking! My house, in comparison to this one would have you in and out in less than five minutes – this house needed time. Our work would never be accomplished in one night, or two. I knew we would be back.

As we left the séance, I was grateful for the small room we ventured up to next. Moderately furnished with a single bed, wardrobe and dressing table, it was quite basic in appearance. I would have put it down as a child's room on my first observation, but observations can be deceiving. People move furniture round and this room was not as it once was. It was also disliked by one member of staff. If someone dislikes going into a room there is always a reason. I found out why this room felt intimidating.

I made myself comfy on a small space of carpet on the floor, my team got comfy too and utilised the remainder of floor space. We began the vigil. I had my back to a tall wardrobe so no one could grab me from behind. Well, you can think that can't you? There are some spirits I wouldn't trust. I heard voices, like someone talking to me, except I couldn't make out what they were saying. I sat in the darkness staring at the bright silver lights dancing across the room. I knew spirit were definitely present. I could feel someone walk close behind me, dipping the floor boards as they passed. I knew that wardrobe shouldn't have been there. I also knew it wasn't my imagination when I heard the whisper of voices. A voice had been captured on my voice recorder belonging to a woman. The voice was saying something that sounded like, 'Get your camera flash away from the window.' Not something any of my team would say. Strange as it sounds, another group of mine were in the building opposite. Their torches shone through the windows as they walked along the corridor. This could have been the reason why spirit wanted us to take our cameras away from the window. Spirit was helping us, only we didn't realise it at the time.

It became obvious as to why my spirit guide, Hannah, had given me the advice she had. She had told me earlier to save the best room till last. We were in room 'x', the last room of the vigil. I didn't altogether feel comfortable. I felt we were not alone and my feelings were right. My team sat in silence in the dark. The room had been used as a gentleman's room throughout its historical period. The conversations that took place would have been addressing government and state matters. I had a feeling as a woman as I shouldn't be in this room, and felt spirit thought this too.

I also had a feeling of being watched, but not by the living. Well, yes them too. But it was the portraits that decorated the walls that didn't feel right. The people in the portraits were uncannily beyond life size. Not your average household picture you could hang on a wall. Besides, you wouldn't have the room for these in a regular house - trust me, you wouldn't. Yet, it wasn't just the size of the portraits within their gold gilded frames that worried me, it was the eyes. The eyes looked as though they were following me. The way the artists had painted them almost looked surreal. The portraits felt haunted.

As the team settled down and the lights switched off trying to see in the dark was impossible. I wanted to hold someone's hand but thought better of it. Who knows where your hand will end up! We were waiting for something to happen when suddenly there were tapping sounds on the window. Well, I knew there couldn't be anybody outside since the room was a floor up from the ground. It did make me and the team jump as we weren't expecting anything to happen. Settling back into our seats, the silence was once again abruptly interrupted by the sound of footsteps. I double checked my team who were all accounted for. The footsteps continued.

A wooden floor outside in the passageway stretched almost the length of the house. A carpet runner covered some of the flooring. Whoever it was outside the room appeared to be very busy, pacing up and down. Not wanting to open the door and venture out for fear of disturbing the energy, we sat and waited, waiting for the energy to move into our room. I thought if this was spirit at work and we went out and disturbed it, we may not hear anything more. I knew the TV monitor was set up in the next room so would capture any anomaly as it occurred.

When nothing further happened we made our way back to the kitchen, our base. Our technical manager needed to visit the dining room to change the video tape. Another team member would accompany him. The dining room was adjacent to room 'x', the 'gentlemen's room. My technical manager, thinking he was being accompanied by another team member behind him set off with a spare tape to make the change. When he entered the room he heard voices but couldn't see anyone. It wasn't till he looked behind him he realised he was alone, well almost. The other team member had unexpectedly got delayed and was not with him. Suffice to say, he didn't feel comfortable. He was right not to feel comfortable and didn't stay any longer than he needed to in changing the tape over.

After a cold and somewhat busy night we collected all our equipment and trigger objects calling time at 05:30am. Back at base and in the kitchen, we concluded during the de-brief how successful the evening had gone. Couldn't explain much, but then that's what makes paranormal 'paranormal' a mystery. No trigger object had moved from its position, which was disappointing.

However, there was other evidential activity that had been taking place. The tape in the dining room had recorded a chair that appeared to have moved out of place. It was a strange phenomenon since one frame showed the chair at the table, then a flicker, followed by the chair positioned away from the table. The dining table would have seated over twenty people. I wondered if the spirit who had been pacing up and down, and whose footsteps were heard had perhaps been preparing dinner.

In the early part of the century a household of this size would have been accustomed to servants waiting on them. I wondered if one still continued to serve. It was an interesting evening and I couldn't help but feel spirit had been busy following us, observing us observing them. I won't be going there for dinner!

Carole Bromley

Haunted Navy

Is the Navy haunted? Investigating a large government run establishment like H.M. Royal Navy wasn't going to be an easy task. Nor was it all in a day's work, as I was to discover. I had heard from my assistant at the time, Bethany, reports of strange goings on at Plymouth Dockyards Naval base. When Bethany asked me to call the Navy and investigate I thought she must be mad, or I was! However, I gave it some considerable thought and made the call. I was ready to do more quality and quantitative research on paranormal phenomena.

I was privileged to have had the expertise and guidance of John J Williamson, F.S.M., D.Sc (H.C), Assoc. Brit.I.R.E.,F.C.G.L.I, founder of *'The Society of Metaphysicians (Hastings)'* and who had been my mentor for some time. The organisation was formed by John whilst in the Royal Air Force and commended by Air Chief Marshal Lord Dowding. The society has used many mystics, mediums and scientists in research projects for over sixty years. I consulted with John on how I could best work on research for the investigation. I needed his expert advice and was delighted when he agreed and endorsed me to represent the Society for research and data collection purposes. His scientific values added to my work and helped keep me calm amongst the various types of energy fields I found myself working in. John has also complemented both my field and mental skills, including those of my strong psychic abilities in the field.

I was also grateful for the advice from Professor Paul who gave me inspiration and guidance on 'How to Succeed', how 'not to give up' and how to put 'facts' into perspective. His words of wisdom helped me through a difficult and arduous period of not just my life, but the investigation and putting the report together.

When I decided it would do no harm to call the Navy I found my timing couldn't have been more perfect. Picking up the phone and dialling the number I was able to speak to a wonderful Commanding Officer who was very helpful. We would also work together for the duration of the project. He told me strange things *had* been occurring and he was seriously considering calling in 'ghost investigators.' He was just as much interested as I was in finding out what was going on. I was glad I called and I was pretty chuffed I had summoned up the courage to make the call. It was going to be an adventure I would never forget. It still haunts me.

I arranged to meet the Commanding Officer for the first time on Saturday 6th March 2004. My Hubby had driven me to Plymouth for the meeting. We would drive back the same day; it was a long way for me to travel. It was also the first time I realised something was wrong with me. I was ill, but didn't know why, or what was causing the illness. I didn't even know it was an illness. I kept putting the bad bouts of diarrhoea down to my not eating adequately. At 5 feet 2 inches my weight of eight stone used to be quite healthy. Now I was losing weight. After several visits to the doctor nothing could be found to be wrong. They were wrong. The not knowing what was wrong didn't help matters. I mean, one day I would be ok, the next I would be violently ill.

I had skipped breakfast before travelling the long distance from London to Plymouth to meet the Commander. I couldn't risk eating when I had to travel. I couldn't eat. It seemed my digestive system would throw out everything I ate and I would be violently sick. If it wasn't coming out one end it was coming out the other! I thought as the doctors couldn't find a cause it must be me. I just had to get on with life, except that life had now become different and more difficult. I would think it would soon resolve itself and tried not worry about it. So, I didn't worry. I carried on as normal, thinking I was normal. But what I had wasn't normal, nor was it nice.

We had to make a few pit stops *en route* to Plymouth, mostly for me to use the loo. I convinced myself I must have a virus and if I stopped eating it would settle down. I was looking forward to meeting the Commanding Officer; I had been liaising with him for many weeks leading up to the initial meeting and the pre-site survey. An upset stomach wouldn't stop me from missing such an important opportunity.

Arriving at the gates of the dockyards I felt relieved, I had a big dislike of travelling. I couldn't believe after the months that had passed I had finally made it. The Navy was a huge place, I hadn't realised how big it actually was. Nonetheless, I wasn't going to be put off with the vastness of area the yards covered. I had a job to do. The Commanding Officer, complete with whiskery grey beard met me at the gate. I took to him the moment I saw him. He was very pleasant, and without any airs or graces. It was also pleasing to know how open-minded he was about the paranormal. Still, I guess after all the unexplained reports about strange goings on he had received from credible sources, it wasn't something he could easily dismiss. I was given a badge to wear as he escorted me to places he had recommended for investigating.

The first place we stopped at was The ' *Master RopeMakers House'*. This house was initially used by the man in charge of *'The Ropery'*. Later would be used as a residence to Dockyard officials, Admiralty Pilots and a Captain. The house, in all its elegance was an 18th century Grade II historic building and built as part of the South Yard *'Ropery'*. For years the building had reputedly been reported as 'haunted'. Some say it is the most 'haunted' house in Plymouth.

The house had stood empty for many years and had many stories to tell, not all were good. The stories didn't bother me but must have caused terrible nightmares for those who having lived at the house had to experience them. One story came from security personnel who claimed to have seen lights on at the house during the night. No one would be brave enough to go inside and switch them off. The Commander had also received reports from naval ratings that had seen dark ghostly figures. The figures would walk past buildings in the dark of the night, disappearing without trace.

The Commander and I walked round to the back of the house and to the small cobbled courtyard. Pausing for breath, I waited in anticipation as the Commander fumbled with his keys trying to open the door. I was aware of the many different types of psychic energies that surrounded not just the house, but the courtyard and garden too. It felt as though a mass of energy had gathered. I can't say that I felt totally comfortable either, but I wasn't worried. There is a difference between feeling uncomfortable and feeling worried. I was uncomfortable.

Looking up at the windows on the top floor I couldn't help feel that the building appeared to be crooked, it didn't stand straight. Of course it did but that's not how I saw it. The feeling I had about this house from the outside wasn't good; I knew I'd get the same feeling about the inside too.

I wanted to get inside. I was glad when the Commander finally opened the door and we were in. Starting on the ground floor we visited each room in turn before working our way up to the attic. My objective was to ensure there would be no obstacles or danger that would affect my team when we came to investigate. We would be working in total darkness. There were no carpets on the floors, only wooden floor boards. It echoed. The rooms were large and spacious, the wallpaper faded or peeling away from where it once hung. The stairs narrow and winding led up to other floors. I didn't like the staircase which stretched four floors up. I felt the presence of spirit walking with me. There were plenty of cupboards in many of the rooms to which children could play 'hide 'n' seek', or, perhaps avoid punishment. We made an inspection of every floor before descending back down the 'haunted' staircase to the ground floor. We left closing the door behind us. I loved this house - it held decades of history and with it many stories to be told; if anyone would listen.

The Commander led the way to the notorious *'Hanging Cell'* where the only remaining working gallows in the United Kingdom remains. In Napoleon's reign many French sailors and criminals lives would be crudely taken away when they fell at the end of a rope. There would be no escape from this cell. Neither would there be any view. The blue heavy iron doors would keep a prisoner safe and secure within its stone walls now painted white. The wooden planks covered half of the top part of the cell; a concrete floor beneath it. The gallows lever large and menacing now stands still and silent. No longer does the *'hangman'* need to condemn anyone to their death. He does not exist.

Allegedly 101 nails were hammered into the walls by some of the prisoners. Though there was little evidence of this, and, only one or two nails remained from what I could see. I could also see why some staff refused to enter the cell. Staff whose job it was to clean the area either didn't stay long, or wouldn't walk through its door. The very nature and purpose of the cell could send some people's imagination running wild. Or, perhaps people, who like me, could sense, or feel real torture and pain.

I found the cell fascinating, nauseating and intimidating, the latter two more so. Looking down from the gallows where the lever was situated made my stomach turn over. The very thought of a rope hanging round someone's neck didn't bear thinking about. Neither did the *finale*, as the boards below a prisoner's feet pulled open on the wrench of the 'hangman's' lever. The poor soul would be left hanging in mid air, his or her neck snapped by the force of the rope. The body would be cut loose to drop onto the hard concrete floor beneath them. The smell of urine, excrement and death was overpowering. It was time to make an exit.

After a long chat with the Commander I left the dockyards and returned home. I was to await a phone call giving me clearance to investigate the two areas I had been shown. Within the week I had got my call and permission to investigate H.M. Royal Navy Dockyards, Plymouth. I had a lot of work to do in recruiting professional people to do the required work. I had just two months leading up to the investigation to organise the work. The investigation would take place in May 2004. It was a huge responsibility, not just for me but for those who would take part in the investigation.

My physical energies during the months leading up to the investigation were totally absorbed in going to work doing my day job. At night I would rush home to structure and plan the investigation. It was all going fairly well until my health deteriorated. I was still ill, my weight had dropped to under six stone and my bones were sticking through my skin. I had to be admitted to hospital for investigations during March. The medical investigations proved fruitless, nothing could be found for the condition I had, nor could I be given medication. Medication is given to treat what is 'known', my condition was 'unknown.' I was used to the 'unknown'. Once again I was on my own with something neither I, nor anyone else could explain.

I still had to go to work and I still had an investigation to plan. My attention focused on a report the Commander had sent me. A family member who at one time resided at the *'Master RopeMakers',* house had sent him a letter. In the letter were details of many paranormal experiences, the contents were quite disturbing. Some members of the family who had personally experienced some events were deceased. It was those still living who were able to pass these experiences on. A few members of the family had expressed an interest in joining the team and the investigation. I agreed with their request as I felt they needed explanations, above all they needed closure.

The report the Commander received told of separate incidents that took place in the *'Master RopeMakers'* house. One incident occurred in the *'scullery'* where one afternoon Mrs Miller had gone to fetch something from the fridge-freezer. This was situated in the corner of the room. As an item was taken out from the fridge there was a sudden feeling of very strong firm hands that gripped her shoulders. Mrs Miller was picked up and thrown hard across the room.

On another occasion Mrs Miller had been confined to bed in the *'front bedroom'* feeling unwell. There had been a fault on the phone line to which she had reported to the phone engineer. When the engineer came to check the phone line he had to go into the bedroom to investigate what the problem was. Mrs Miller stood in front of the dressing room table, her husband by her side when the dressing table appeared to have been given a hard push and toppled over. It took both Mr & Mrs Miller a lot of strength to upright it again because it seemed extremely heavy. Mrs Miller believed the engineer to be in the room at the time.

Another incident in the house happened when Mrs Miller was coming down the stairs, she had always felt a presence in this area. On one occasion she felt someone's hands on her shoulders trying to push her over.

Unfortunately, one of her daughter's was, by an unknown force, pushed down the stairs.

The biggest mystery in the letter was connected to the family's mongrel dog called *'Blackie'*. Mr Miller had entered the kitchen one morning when he found the walls and floor covered in blood. It was as if *'Blackie'* had been in a fight with something because a sheet of Formica on the window sill was covered in teeth marks and blood stains. The dog was taken to the vets for a check up but nothing was seen to suggest any blood came from him.

I pondered over the contents of this letter for many weeks and I didn't like what I had read. It must have been very disturbing for the family to have lived with whatever entity was haunting them. My heart felt for them.

Knowing the investigation was going to be for a full weekend and fast approaching I was getting increasingly concerned about my health. Nothing I took would help my condition. I had worked exceptionally hard organising and getting everyone ready. Pulling out was not an option. I should have pulled out but I would have let a lot of people down, including myself. I don't like letting people down. The first investigation went ahead.

Thursday 27th May, 2004. I arrived with Hubby at the bed & breakfast hotel in Plymouth. I was to meet the Commanding officer later in the day to re-inspect the two locations to be investigated. Most of the team would also be staying at the same hotel when they arrived, some would meet up the following day. I didn't know it at the time, nor had the thought crossed my mind but the *'Ghost Investigation'* was to attract a substantial amount of media interest. It became of interest in many parts of the world, from New York to S. Africa, Canada, India and Spain, not to mention the UK. I'd been invited to do interviews for national newspapers, radio stations and television networks. I hadn't realised how exhausting all the interviews would be. I did nominate other members of the team to speak to some of the media. But for me, it was a big mistake to fit so much into such a small window of time.

By Friday my energies were diminishing. I wasn't eating and felt drained; I didn't want anyone to know just how ill I was and tried not to show it. Breakfast was fine, but I still couldn't keep what I had consumed in. I had frequent visits to the loo and no sleep the night before. It *had* been a big mistake to do so many interviews the day before.

I arrived at the dockyards with the team on Friday at 6:30pm. It was only a short distance from our hotel, I was grateful for this. Whilst I had been told we were to investigate two buildings a little voice told me different; I was told by Hannah my spirit guide there was going to three. She was right the Commander decided at the last minute to add an extra building, The *'Ropery'*. It didn't make any difference; we would shorten vigils in the other two locations; The *'Master RopeMaker's'* House and the *'Hanging Cell'*.

I was interested to see how the different types of people I had chosen to do the work required on a 'paranormal' (beyond the range of normal or scientific explanation) level addressed the investigation as a whole. One team consisted of a multitude of skilled individuals including psychics, mediums, healers, sceptics, a scientist as well as navy civilians. The other team consisted of paranormal report investigators invited to work alongside the team made up of mediums. The reason for such a wide range of personnel was to see if a combination of skills in a unit would produce results that would be any different. Some people observed and perceived certain events whilst others did not.

It was important that the Law of Unity existed during the investigation and the work ahead, but in some cases it could not exist due to the different skills people worked with. It was also due to the different dimensions (a space having its own limitations) that some team members were able to enter into a higher state of consciousness, compared to those who were, in fact limited by their own restrictions to reach a higher state of awareness. There was no possibility that those who were restricted to observing events would be able to work with or communicate with other energy forces.

The mediums and members of the team I chose to work alongside me and as part of the team knew the work was not going to be easy. This was due to the vast amount of negative energy forms present and the long hours ahead. All of which proved physically draining to some. The team were also working with not only physical energies but non-physical negative energies.

The *'Master RopeMakers'* house was the first to be investigated. But, as the evening went on, so did my frequent visits to the loo. I barely managed to complete the night. I had to head back to the hotel leaving the team to continue without me. It was a hard decision but I served no purpose, I was in too much pain. The next morning Hubby and I packed our bags. I made my apologies and left the team to continue the work and the investigation. Hubby rushed me straight to our local hospital.

I was kept in overnight and accused by the doctor of causing my weight disorder; I was now under six stone. I was angry with the doctor and his obvious misdiagnosis. There was no way I was anorexic, but looking at me you'd think different. I was transferred to another hospital and to the consultant I was previously under in March. He investigated me again. He still couldn't find anything. He even suggested I was stressed due to the amount of public and media attention I had got during the course of the weekend. He kept me in for further observation and tests.

I had been receiving calls whilst in hospital from the team telling me about the investigation at the dockyards. I had been receiving calls from the media too wanting to interview me. I couldn't give interviews and was extremely disappointed I couldn't be at the dockyards. The consultant, puzzled by my condition eventually found what was wrong. It was a rare bowel disease that could only be found under a microscope. I was relieved and pleased. Pleased that I could now be treated, it wasn't life threatening but it did change my way of life and my diet.

Nothing could compensate for my absence from the investigation, I was heart-broken. All the hard work I had done to put it together was now worthless to me. I had to stay in hospital for almost a week. There were hordes of people trying to get hold of me. By the time I got out everything was over. Everyone had a good time, all except me. The only thing left for me to do when I had fully recovered was to put the report together from the information gathered by the team. The report relied heavily on their input.

From the data analysis conducted after the investigation, it was reported eleven people felt the floor in the front bedroom of the house shaking. Ten people felt the house to have a moving sensation. Seven people reported their legs feeling heavy. There were unexplained occurrences on the stairs; such as the stairs appearing to move. Some people had felt a slap to the side of their face. Six people felt the presence of a young girl. Mediums were aware of children playing inside and outside of the house. Five people felt the presence of a young boy. Residue energies of fear and anger in the house were reported by many of the mediums. Four people disliked the energy in the kitchen. Some mediums reported they felt female adults were subject to domestic violence. Three people felt the taste of sulphur in their mouth. Some mediums heard screams and felt pushing sensations. Two people tried to exit a room but found the door was jammed. Animals were thought to be buried in the garden. Sickness and nausea sensations were sensed from feelings of buried human remains in the garden.

A substantial amount of phenomena was reported that could not be explained. Besides the strange phenomena some people were experiencing in the 'Master RopeMakers' House, the 'Hanging Cell' had phenomena of its own. Some team members were showing physical signs of stress, including one Navy civilian who cried out in pain and had to leave the cell.

When she stood up it was difficult for her to walk, instead she found herself limping as she headed towards the door. This was by far a strange phenomenon. The TV monitor flickered when someone from the team asked spirit to show itself. Unexplained interference was recorded on the TV monitor. A vast amount of orb activity was taking place and recorded. Audible sounds of footsteps were physically heard. There were also clinking noises and flashes of white light that could not be explained. A flash of yellow light appeared in the cell followed by a dark shadowy figure moving on one side of the wall. There was so much going on in the cell it was unfortunate I missed it all due to my acute illness when I had to rush home to London.

I was feeling a little better when we returned to the Navy for our second visit on Friday 10th & Saturday 11th September, 2004. I decided not to invite the paranormal support team whom I had invited on our first visit, much to their disappointment. The reason why I felt the paranormal support team would not be required was because they could not work on a psychic level. Their skills were not of the same as those of mediums. They could not assist in working with psychic energies at the areas we had previously investigated.

During this visit we were invited to take part in the filming of a BBC documentary called 'Shipmates, Raising the Dead', produced and directed by Chris Tyrell. I hadn't fully recovered medically from my last visit in May and was still only weighing in at six stone. The use of physical energy whilst working with a team of twenty seven people would be draining. I had a lot of responsibility in people to take care of. There was also the mass of non physical energies I had to work with too.

When the team set up equipment in the *'Hanging Cell'* on Friday night for our first vigil, we noticed strange things were happening. The TV screen showed frequent interference for no logical reason. Two large bangs were heard that could not be explained. Team members' faces itched constantly. A mass of spiritual energy was seen to superimpose itself (transfiguration) on the face of one non-sensitive team member. This energy made her face look distorted. Some members of the team experienced a stabbing sensation in the back of the neck. The temperature appeared to fluctuate and change periodically, sometimes dropping quite rapidly. Camera batteries were consistently drained and being replaced, but not through usage as new batteries would also fail to work.

Saturday evening the team commenced a vigil in the reputedly haunted *'Master RopeMaker's House'*. We used and set up equipment that consisted of: Motion detectors, TV recorders and CCTV cameras with night vision technology that would record activity in the dark. We had set trigger objects in almost every room of the house. Infra red temperature readings had been taken intermittently. We used the Tri-Corder *Natural* EMF Meter to monitor electronic fields. The EMF can detect changes in extremely weak static (DC or "natural") electric and magnetic fields. The team certainly missed no opportunity in setting up a variety of experiments.

When we all gathered upstairs to prepare for a séance I walked into one room and into an energy that didn't want us there. I was aware of a male energy cursing at me telling me *he* didn't want us there. I cursed back telling him, 'I'm going to leave this room now but when I come back in a few minutes I want you to be more polite to me'. After a few minutes I re-entered the room and the energy felt better. I moved the team in to start the séance.

Before the séance started some members of the team reported to feel the staircase had a moving sensation. Reports of a female spirit figure were seen rushing down the stairs. Claims of children's voices were heard. Temperature fluctuations were consistent. Many things were going on that could not be physically explained. However, when the team started the séance it appeared to cause all sorts of problems. Sat in a circle on the hard wooden floor boards and in total darkness gave spirit a good opportunity to misbehave. As if they hadn't already! Some members of the team reported the feeling of someone touching their ears yet everyone was holding hands. Besides, if anyone did touch someone's ears everyone would know since the team was wearing glow-in-the-dark bangles on their wrists.

Doing battle with one male spirit was hard work for me. Prior to his arrival a little girl had come and stood in the circle. She was wearing a white linen nightgown and crying. I was just about to guide her into the light when the male spirit appeared by my side. He started walking round me but I took no notice. I wanted to put the little child into the light. He would prevent me from doing this as he took her hand and pushed her against the wall. This was new I hadn't seen this happen before. I found myself arguing with him to let her go but he was adamant she was his. She wasn't his and she certainly didn't like him, neither did I. I managed to manoeuvre the psychic energies that had formed in the circle to make a tunnel of light for the little girl to enter. Using my own psychic energy I kept the man away from her, giving myself a headache in the process. The little girl crossed over, much to the male spirits annoyance.

Just as that battle had ended another one began. One of the medium's who was clearly in distress and on the verge of collapse shouted at me, 'Goldy, get me out.' I pulled her up from the floor and pushed her outside the room where she made a full recovery. An unexplained energy force had impressed itself on her and caused her to react the way she did. There was so much going on in the house with different team members reporting different forms of phenomena, it was interesting to say the least. I certainly had my work cut out!

After we closed the séance upstairs we set up vigils in rooms on the ground floor. Two team members sat in an adjoining room to one of the vigils to monitor activities that were being recorded. When I went to check on the two team members who had been monitoring the activity, they reported having experienced activity of their own. Whilst one of the team was monitoring the TV she was aware of something going on with her foot. Her shoe lace was slowly being untied! Two team members entered two different rooms adjacent to one another at the same time and experienced something similar to walking into a spider's web. They had to brush their faces off.

All was going really well so far, but it was time to move onto another building and another vigil. Our next location to investigate was The *'Ropery'*, a building used as a major producer of rope and cordage for the whole Navy up until March 1941. Sadly, due to bomb damage from two world wars production in the *'Ropery'* ceased. The energies in this location had a very negative feeling; this made me feel slightly uncomfortable as I made my way through the entrance of the brick building. The silence was daunting but it didn't put me off walking down the long stretch of the building.

I remember being drawn in one direction that would take me deeper into the *'Ropery'*. I was looking for a good place to hold a séance and needed to feel the energies. As I walked along the stone passageway I was aware of a spirit and pointed to its location as I mentioned this to my colleague. An Orb was captured in a photo that supported my claim. Some of my team members decided to investigate the energies at the other end of the *'Ropery'* and in the opposite direction to where I was heading. I told Chris, the Producer, the direction I was walking in appeared to be the better one as it felt 'uneasy.' Stupid thing to say I know but I was there to do a job and could only do it if the energies were there to work with. It wasn't long before the rest of the team headed my way and we agreed the spot I had chosen would be the better option. (When investigating the paranormal it always makes sense to head in the direction where you feel it to be uncomfortable as the chances of something strange occurring could be better).

We all gathered chairs and sat in a circle whilst two mediums went into trance. During the trance I noticed the Producer's Assistant, Priscilla, moving uncomfortably in her chair. As she moved I could see something wasn't right so I got up and stood behind her putting my hands on her shoulders. At first I thought perhaps she was nervous and after a few minutes I sat back down. However, Priscilla was still moving uncomfortably in her chair when I noticed her eyes were staring straight at me, as though I had done something wrong. I hadn't done anything wrong but her breathing started to get quite rapid and knew this was wrong. I looked round at the other team members and indicated I would take her outside. I grabbed her arm so she stood up and started to walk her towards the door. As we walked towards the door which was almost at the far end of the building Priscilla started screaming. I pushed her to the side of the building against the wall and she burst out laughing very loud. This I knew wasn't Priscilla, she started speaking to me in a foreign language which I couldn't understand; she wasn't making any sense. I hurried her towards the door as quick as I could, at the same time trying to attract one of the team members by waving at them. It was a long stretch of building for anyone to notice me waving. Nobody did.

Once outside I propped her on the rail of the concrete staircase, she was still laughing and continuing to speak in a foreign language. I stood there holding her, hoping and praying someone in my team would come out. I asked Priscilla what her name was as it was obvious she wasn't the person we knew. She was shouting 'Nina! Nina! Nina!' Her eyes were chillingly open wide as she stared at me. I thought she was going to push me over the rail but instead she climbed up and started leaning over it. I hung onto her jumper and asked her who 'Nina' was and Priscilla replied, 'My wife, my wife!' It was at this point another team member came out and was able to help me get her safely away from the rail and down the steps. We walked her up and down outside the building for some time.

I told the team member to go back inside and try to wind down the séance. I knew it was something that should not be done but under the circumstances felt necessary. I didn't want anyone else going 'under'. Without the energies of the team I knew the energies of the mass of spirits that had gathered would diminish. Chris, the producer came outside but did not film the event; our concern was to get rid of the spirit that had possessed his assistant. It took over five hours before Priscilla came back to herself. It took another week for Priscilla to recover, the experience left her with a nasty mouth full of ulcers.

Priscilla wasn't the only one contaminated and affected by the energy of this spirit; another team member who had sat next to her was behaving a little strange too. Some of the mediums worked quickly on cleansing off the energy attached to her and she recovered.

I had also taken on some of the energy myself as I remember staring at people and being aware of a male figure. It was very surreal, it was like slow motion watching the world go round only I wasn't part of it. I was somewhere different but I wasn't. It's hard to explain but that's how I felt. It began when I visited the toilet and couldn't move. I was aware of an energy belonging to a man. I can't remember what I said but the other mediums made sure he wasn't going to stay. They worked on cleansing my energies too but it took me some time to recover, I couldn't participate in the last séance which was held in the *'Hanging Cell'*. I had no energy left in me. The attachment of the male spirit was not a nice experience at all; I would never allow spirit to use me in that way again. I have since learnt to be in better control of the 'dead'! My energies had been contaminated with the negative entity when I placed my hands on Priscilla's shoulders. I can only try to explain this transferral of energy by a way of if you touch someone you get what people call an 'electric shock'.

No one was sure what had happened in this location, or why Priscilla suddenly became possessed by the disturbed spirit. Chris the producer reported, 'I still cannot explain what happened that night – neither can Priscilla, but, despite my misgivings about the ghost-trapping in the 'Rope master's House, I still would not say with any certainty that we did not, that night, have close contact with the spirit of a dead French sailor.' (Terrill, C, 2005).

I'm not sure where the 'French Sailor' came from but it was a very interesting weekend. I know I learned and experienced a great deal and I know everyone else did too. But, the weekend wasn't over yet. The Commander had asked if we could exhibit our findings at their open day the very next day. I had brought with me photographs from our last visit and could use video materials we had recorded over the weekend. I agreed; it would be good to show the general public our findings so arranged for some team members to join me at the event.

It was hard finding interested parties, especially as we had all been up working for two solid nights running. Many of us, including myself had only up to three hours sleep but we didn't want to disappoint. I'm glad some of us made it as there was quite a good turnout from the public, all showing a keen interest in the work we had displayed. I was pleased I had participated fully this time. Unlike my last visit, I wasn't trying to run an investigation from my hospital bedside!

This investigation was initially meant to be private, but with press and media interest it soon became very public. There were stories and reports featured in: The Telegraph; The Sun; News of the World; Evening Herald; Sunday Independent; Western Morning News; Daily Express; Fate

& Fortune Magazine; Psychic News; BBC World Service; Radio Five Live; Radio Four; British Forces Radio; Talksport Radio; The Canadian Broadcasting Corporation; Spanish Radio; Pirate FM; Radio Devon; Radio Cornwall; Plymouth Sounds; BBC Breakfast News; Spotlight; ITV Carlton and Sky News. The whole experience was phenomenal but not one I would repeat again.

In some of our evidence a team member using my camera captured an image of a ghostly figure looking out of a window in Bonaventura House. This location was our base on the first visit. Further paranormal activity happened when the team was in the *'Hanging Cell'* and the fire alarm went off. No one had heard the alarm trigger. We only found out about the incident when a naval rating reported that it was showing up in the system - in a building some distance from the Cell.

Overall, the weekend was extremely exhausting and I hadn't managed to eat properly due to finding time; at least I was able to participate. My function was to monitor the events, ensure all team members were safe, assist in recording the documentary, direct the team in their given tasks and check equipment. As the organiser, I never really had quality time to use my psychic or mediumistic skills to my full potential; I was always too busy doing other things.

One of our missions was accomplished in the crossing over of many 'lost souls' into the light of God the divine spirit. These souls could rest and be re-united with their loved ones on the other side. However, not all spirit energies wanted to cross over and will remain present until they decide otherwise.

It wasn't just strange things going on at the naval base that concerned me. Whilst working on the report I encountered the unexplained occurrences of two of my television sets breaking down. An electric iron had to be replaced. My home phone broke and ceased to work and needed to be replaced. My husband's mobile kept switching itself on for no reason. Light bulbs kept blowing in my home as well as immense electrical fluctuations with the lights. My computer equipment failed to function and my printer broke. Coincidence? Is there such a thing?

The report I compiled and submitted to the Commanding Officer was in total 132 pages long. Therefore, it has not been possible to report everything here. Writing the report took many months of total commitment and dedication. Every hour I had available after my 9-5+ job I made sure I gave qualitative and quantitative time to research what had been investigated. Every weekend was spent analysing materials taken from the investigation. Viewing video footage twice and listening to EVP's (electronic voice phenomena) twice kept me busy. I also viewed video footage in order to research and analyse an orb study. The study indicated where Orb's entered and exited a room. The pattern of the Orbs was also something I was very much interested in.

The buildings in the South Yard were to become part of the naval base's museum. Whether this has or will happen I cannot say for certain. However, in answer to my question in the first sentence of this chapter, 'Is the Navy Haunted'? Without a doubt there was certainly a lot of phenomena that could not be explained.

'Simon'

My Hubby may be sceptic but explaining to him how we have a son in the Spirit world called 'Simon' would not fit in with his rationale. We wanted a baby but nothing was happening. We had thought about and read about IVF (In vitro-fertilisation) and decided that would be our best route. Whatever the costs we would give the IVF at least one attempt or we would regret not having tried.

It was a very difficult decision to make since we would have to prepare for the procedure that would either bless us with a child of our own, or we would have to prepare for the worst. It was a 50/50 chance we had to take. How do you prepare for the worst? How do you prepare for the prospect of living a life without a family? We so much wanted a family.

We had both undergone what can only be described as the most intimate procedures in preparing for IVF at the hospital. We had a good team of consultants which made the process a little easier to work with. Yet, in our minds we couldn't help but think if it would work or not. It was a chance we had had to take. It didn't matter how much it cost us financially, we were prepared to take a risk.

I had gone through the ordeal of stabbing myself daily with the injections I had to make and when the day had arrived for the final procedure, the implant of the 'egg'. It was August 11th 1999. It was the day of the total eclipse. This was a special eclipse of the sun as it only happened once every eighty years. The calendar dates also added up to No.11, August, the eight month, 11th the date, 1999. Working this date out in numerology would look like; $8+1+1+1+9+9+9 = 38$, $3+8 = 11$.

I dreaded the intrusive procedure and both of us were nervous of the outcome. I was uncomfortable about the calendar date, and the time, as the eclipse was going to occur at 11:11am. As much as I tried I couldn't get the date changed, everything had to happen in synchronicity with the procedure. I had *one* egg (my baby) and a 1% chance the IVF would work. I had my doubts. I was in and out of the theatre in no time.

I returned from theatre about 11.00am when I saw people gathering outside close to my window. Everyone was wearing their special 3D glasses and waiting for the eclipse to occur and move over the sun. It was a strange phenomenon to witness as the morning light changed to an eerie darkness. The number 11 has for me has always been unlucky, I see the number quite often and every time it comes up I get anxious. I often wonder if it is because of the voices I had heard on the eve of my sister's passing when I was 11 years old. I wonder if it was something to do with the date and time of the IVF. I will always wonder.

My husband brought me a dozen red roses to cheer me up as we waited anxiously for the IVF to work. I couldn't sleep. I cannot begin to tell you how painful those two weeks were in waiting to see if we had a child. Each day I looked at the roses and each day one would die. Eleven roses died and only one survived. I knew in my heart the procedure had not worked. Words cannot describe how devastated we were.

Two years later and early one evening I sat in my chair in front of the fire all alone. I felt sad as I thought about 'Simon', the baby we had lost. I know it wasn't my fault he couldn't be born to the earth plane, neither was it his. It wasn't the right time; his spirit wasn't ready to be born. I didn't know how I could go on believing in spirit. I didn't know how I could go on working for spirit either, I felt so let down.

As I was thinking of Simon I felt a cold breeze and a light pressure around my feet. The coldness moved up to my knee and continued to rise up to my neck. I knew straight away it was the energy of a spirit, and I knew who the energy belonged to. It was the spirit of my son 'Simon'. As my unborn baby snuggled up to me and hugged me he told me, 'Mummy, please don't give up.' He told me he loved me, he told me spirit *needed* me. As I sat listening to the words of my baby tears streamed down my face. I realised I would never physically hold my own baby. I so much wanted to hold him. I realised I would never be a 'Mother'. I so much wanted to be a Mother. Most of all, I realised my son had not died; he had survived and lives on, to me that was all that mattered. Working with those in the spirit world is all that mattered. I would never like red roses again.

I was to see our son 'Simon' again when I was learning the rune stones. I was woken up in the middle of night to see a vision of a small boy standing by the side of my bed. He whispered his name to me, but he didn't need to. I noticed in his hands he was holding a bag of runes, the same bag of runes that belonged to me. He smiled cheekily at me as he took some stones out of the bag and handed them to me. I smiled back at him, thanked him and he turned and left. I know he is never far away; he's still our son and my love for our son lives on.

Haunted Memories

Although I thoroughly enjoy investigating the paranormal I still had a day job to do. I couldn't give up my job because the University had become part of my life for over eight years. I loved going to work, I always learnt something. I adored being amongst people from different nationalities, so working in a multi-cultural environment was a beautiful experience in itself.

I have never really been very good at keeping jobs; I would either leave or be made redundant. Nothing has changed since I have been advised of the possibility of redundancy three times now, each time some miracle saves me. My time and money spent on my social science Open University degree course I had to abandon half way through, I foresaw that my job situation would change. Nonetheless, I know mum was happy for me to have settled down at last, I know she was also proud of me, proud that I worked in a bit of a posh environment. Well, that's what she thought and I suppose she was right, it was a bit posh.

I was working at the University when mum died. It was just another normal day when I was busy getting ready for work. Glancing over at Mum I thought she didn't look too well. I had recently been thinking of taking her out more. I wanted to do more things with her, involve her in my life more, but I never found the time. I was always too engrossed in working on research or investigation reports. I was seeing people who wanted a reading but often didn't really *need* a reading.

Mum was seventy eight and the kind of person who was very active, she always had to be doing things. I thought I would ask her when I returned home from work if she was ok. This was a big mistake. I should have asked her then and there before I left for work.

My cab had arrived and I said to Mum as she trotted off up the stairs, 'See you later', as I did every morning. I arrived at work and sat at my desk when I heard a voice whisper in my ear, 'Give Mum your mobile number.' I felt irritated and couldn't think of anything else except giving

Mum my new number. I had been meaning to give it her but kept forgetting.

There were no indications from spirit about my mum's future. Spirit did not tell me of the massive heart attack she would endure. Even if I did know I could not have stopped it from happening. But I didn't know and I wasn't prepared. When it's our turn to go it's not a case of 'if' it's a case of 'when.' Whether we like it or not, it's not our choice to make, neither is it a date we can schedule in our diary. It's not like we can look at a calendar and say, 'Sorry, not dying today, I'm too busy!

Time is a funny phenomenon, we all set our clocks and calendars by it, we are all governed by dates, years and months aren't we? July 12th 2005 should have been an ordinary working day for me but it wasn't. Instead it would be a special day for both Mum and me for the rest of our lives.

I was kicking myself as I sat in my office irritated by not giving Mum my mobile number. I was just about to call her when the phone rang and it was my mum's sister, she was shouting at me to get to the hospital. I didn't finish listening to the call but instead hung up. I grabbed my mobile phone and desperately tried to figure out how it worked. I was panicking as I tried to call Hubby.

Fortunately, Val in the adjoining office had over heard my panic and came running out asking if everything was ok. Obviously not, I threw the mobile phone at her and asked her to find Hubby's number, I was shaking. She found me the number and I called Hubby and told him to pick me up. I had just caught him as he was closing the front door to go to work.

While I was waiting for him to pick me up Val showed me how to use the directory on my mobile. I was able to find the phone numbers of my brothers and called them one by one telling them to go to the hospital. I knew we were all thinking along the same lines, that it was serious.

I was the first to arrive at the hospital and a nurse directed me to a side room. I knew I wasn't going to see Mum alive. I kept hoping and praying I was very wrong, only I wasn't. My brothers arrived shortly before my nephews, nieces, and other family members. We gathered into a tiny room and were told Mum had died.

Mum was a fighter and not one to be ill, but she couldn't fight a heart attack and didn't stand a chance. The doctor came and sat me on a chair and explained what they had done to try to save her. They had linked her up to machinery where they had tried resuscitation, drugs and everything else but nothing worked. The ambulance had transported her from the hairdressers where she had suffered the heart attack. I know she would be kicking herself at not having had her hair done first. A trip to the salon every Tuesday was the highlight of her week.

The doctor offered to stay with us but I declined telling him he had a job to do and other people needed him more than my family. He looked at me relatively puzzled by my dismissal of him and asked if I was sure. I was sure, there was nothing more he could do; his team had done their best.

I went into a quite little room where Mum had been wheeled and looked down at her as she laid on the bed, quiet, still and peaceful. I cried as I asked the Angels to make sure she crossed over into the white light. I said a prayer and as I looked at her I could have sworn I saw the corner of her bottom lip move. At the end of the prayer I told her, 'I love you Mum,' something I hadn't told her for years. I could have done but never found the time.

Looking at Mum I could have sworn she spoke to me as her bottom lip moved as though she was speaking back to me the words, 'I love you too.' Her lips were blue, she wasn't going to sit up and talk like you would expect, or complain of any pain. She wasn't coming back.

It was the end of an era for my mum and me. Except now, there is just me and the memories that I hold and have shared with Mum. I will always remember the good times, the bad times, the struggles and the survival of a single Mum with five kids.

Hubby and I, along with Mum had decided to buy the house from the Council, something we had pondered over for years. The sale was almost complete except for one final signature which Mum hadn't done. I didn't know what was worse at the time, fighting the spirits or wrestling with the Council. The Council tried to take the house back and told us the house should go to a family. I argued the house had been part of my life since my early child hood; I was part of a family. They wanted to stop the sale. It would have been different if we had kids.

I had lived in the house for almost thirty years on and off and now I was about to see a chapter of my life taken away. I had to take charge and fight for what was mine, but it wasn't mine. I didn't own the house yet.

I was angry with the Council and thought that it made no difference that Mum wasn't here. They knew how old she was when we applied to buy the house, not that age had anything to do with it. There's no age limit on death.

I made several calls to the council offices, went to my MP, all to no avail, it was the same old story, 'You don't have any children.', is something they may as well have said but didn't come right out and say it. How could I move home after living in the same place with the same people for so many years? How could I move knowing memories of my life would be wiped away and I would perhaps forget how my life was? I wasn't having any of it. I didn't want to start again in any old place the Council deemed suitable for our needs. We had our own needs too. I wasn't going to be discriminated against.

I was at my wits end and I hadn't got over losing Mum when I informed the Council of her passing. I was being honest and letting them know the situation. I got no sympathy or empathy, not that I wanted any. I was a door number occupying a piece of collateral to them, I wasn't a human being. Professor Paul was concerned about the lack of co-operation I was getting from the Councillor. Every day for weeks I called them to see if the house was ours and every day I got the same answer, 'We are still working on it.

Professor Paul made a call to the Council himself, I don't know what he said but soon after his call I got one myself. A Councillor told me to go to the Council office with proof of identification and the house would be signed over with immediate effect. I remember asking Professor Paul who on earth they thought they had been writing to for the last two and a half years! It didn't matter, the house was mine and Val, my work colleague very kindly drove me to the place where I produced proof of who I was.

A Councillor knocked on my door the following evening with a letter of confirmation advising me I was now the tenant of the house. If we had lost the house I could guarantee anyone taking it over would feel a little.... haunted!

If Mum had signed the final form perhaps things may have been different, or would they? Paperwork was the least of my problems since I soon had to suffer the ordeal of visiting Mum at the funeral parlour. The visit was to be a very painful experience; words cannot describe my feelings as there are no words to describe them. To me Mum still looked beautiful and peaceful. I couldn't hear any voices from the other side, but I did hear my own voice.

My voice was telling her how sorry I was I didn't spend enough time with her. I could hear myself telling her how I would give her all the time in the world, if she would only come back. She wasn't coming back and now it was 'too late to say sorry'. I could have said it so many times but there was never enough time. Yet, there is always time if we make the effort.

I had written a letter apologising for many things throughout our lives together, apologising for what I should have done for her but didn't. It was too late now. I gave her photos of her family and the pets to take with her, not that she needed them but I didn't want to send her away empty handed. I reached out and touched her hand, feeling the coldness of it. I wanted to kiss her face but couldn't, the pain was too much. I placed the red rose I had bought her gently at her feet inside her coffin, she liked red roses. My voice was speaking to her telepathically so as not to disturb anyone. I know she heard me. My voice was saying to her 'if only' this and 'if only' that. Yes, if only.

Now I make time for my family. I have learned to enjoy being with my Hubby and my pets again. I have found time for them in my life where I had not before. I always felt I was on beck and call to everyone and anyone, morning, noon and night. I never had time for those who mattered most to me. It was such a small change to make finding time to be with my family but it was one change I know I will never regret. Life is very precious, we should use it wisely.

I wanted Mum to speak to me, wanted to hear her voice again, I wanted her to be at home when I returned from the funeral parlour, but she wouldn't be there. Sometimes I would glance under the bedroom door of her room and could have sworn I saw a shadow moving beneath the door, except it isn't her room now, Mum's room, she's passed over. But it is her room, she is still here and I know I saw the light on in her room on one recent visit to the bathroom. I wouldn't go in and turn it off; I was scared; scared in case I might see her sitting there on her bed acting as though nothing had happened. I didn't want to see her, well not yet anyway. I wasn't ready and I wasn't over her passing. In fact I was annoyed she had gone, there was still so much to do, so much I had wanted to say to her and give her.

Mum knew how much I loved my spiritual work and I knew she was proud of me, people would tell her how I had helped them. Mum liked that in people, anyone who could help anyone was a good person in her book. She knew I helped people but not the same way she did, but it didn't matter because by helping others she knew I was doing right by her.

I felt guilty with haunted memories of the months and years I had spent doing my research, not giving Mum enough attention. I was too engrossed in looking for answers on the paranormal and fighting off those who were looking for frauds. I was fighting those who had nothing better to do than look for the bad in people. It is only now I have become to realise that I have nothing to prove to anyone except to Mum. I believe I am now doing that in 'The Living Spirit'.

I know mum watches over me, I know she is amongst her family. The Angels look after her now. She fits in well in *heaven*.

The Researcher

In this big wide Universe there are Scientists, Parapsychologists, Researchers and others, ready and willing to do battle with those who are of 'mediumistic' genre. Good for them. I hope they keep up with the ever growing breed of psychics, mediums and those who have been witness to something paranormal. If only they could keep up with those of us who have witnessed something paranormal, but they can't. Since the number of people who believe they have experienced a ghost, apparition or spiritual communication heavily outweighs the number of those who attempt to research the belief system of others.

Academics have consistently argued, and counter-argued with one another on the subject of psychic functioning, often with conflicting results. You only have to search for what has been scientifically written and you will find how researchers are openly critical to one another. No matter though, this is a 'natural' phenomenon in the world of academia. Research is about arguments. Research into the paranormal is a growing and competitive market. Yet, whilst scientists are battling it out in the field of the paranormal, trying to find evidence, there are a multitude of people experiencing unexplained phenomenon on a daily basis. That's why I feel it is important for science and research to keep up with the increasing psychic phenomenon trends.

The world of psychic phenomenon is undoubtedly moving forward. In comparison with the world of paranormal science, this apparently appears to be stuck in a time-warp. After hundreds of years of research, it has proved difficult to find the truth related to psychic functioning. Or, perhaps the truth has been found. Scientists will agree to disagree in their truth to find something more than the human mind can comprehend. But, are they closer to finding the truth? More important, who can we trust to deliver the truth? Whose research is right, and whose research is wrong? Is there a right way to research psychic and paranormal phenomena?

Millions of 'normal' people who claim to witness something related to the paranormal are often dismissed by scientists. The only scientific explanation these types of people are offered will purport to 'seeing things' or 'hallucinating'. If a person is a psychic or a medium, the scientific explanation could be referred to something more fraudulent. Yet, you do not have to be a psychic or a medium to be witness to a strange phenomenon.

However, to my knowledge there has been no quantitative scientific evidence available to disprove the theory of an afterlife, or that a medium is talking to the 'dead'. Scientists cannot prove there is no after life, or can they? Some have tried to offer proof; some have tried to mask the truth. Yet, as scientists go, who can we really trust? Who can we really believe to publish the truth? The area of parapsychology seems to be the biggest field in investigating mediums and the paranormal. But, can the area of parapsychology as a science prove the 'medium', does not communicate with the 'dead'? Can the area of parapsychology really find evidence of the paranormal? More importantly, can parapsychologists prove a multitude of 'normal' people are not hallucinating, hearing or seeing things? Can 'normal' people argue the science, or even dare to argue?

My view accepts "In a variety of forms and through the ages it has been an evident truth that the more you know, the more you know you do not know. In the search for knowledge it also soon becomes apparent that what is known is a very small part of what we do not know. Our five senses plus a battery of methods, processes and procedures are constantly extending our knowledge, and hence perversely increasing the size of the unknown. And yet ... when it comes to the unknown, we attempt to investigate using the well-worn methods, processes and procedures that have aided in improving our knowledge, but which have not actually made a dent in reducing the unknown. It seems to us that whatever it is that remains to be discovered will require new methods, processes and procedures to be applied since clearly our current methods, processes and procedures have not. So for example, when investigating the paranormal, scientists are likely to observe unusual activities as does everyone else, but because with their equipment they have not be able to identify or even register the existence of the activities, go on to conclude that there is nothing there. Surely a better concluding observation is that the equipment may be inappropriate to the task?" *(Ray J Paul, 2006)*.

Many parapsychologists have tested mediums, published papers and hosted seminars on the subject, each trying to convince themselves and the public there are no 'dead'. John Williamson, (D.Sc), Founder of the Society of Metaphysicians once told me 'No person, no matter how well educated, especially those limited by that formal qualification, can be aware of the wonderful world of total manifestation beyond the human and limited level'. I also know what he meant when he said 'It takes a 'leap of faith' a 'leap in the dark', to become open to and aware of things *beyond* our physical conditioning and life'.

I, we, rely on those with qualifications to examine that of which needs to be fully understood. So, without holding any formal qualifications myself, my argument is based on the interpretations of communications received through a medium from the 'dead'. My argument is based on the way mediums are 'tested' and their messages 'interpreted' by the use of parapsychology that causes me a problem. For me, there is a bit missing. It's the bit between the 'dead' who are able to give evidence of an afterlife, and the bit between the medium demonstrating communications from the 'dead'.

The communication from the 'dead' has to come from somewhere, but where? And, how is this possible? What is the area that allows a medium, or a person who does not have mediumistic abilities the possibility to witness strange phenomena? So, given all this, what area of science should examine this field? And, is parapsychology the science to examine psychic and paranormal functioning?

My intention is to explore the concept of how I understand the subject of parapsychology as a hypothesis for testing psychics, mediums and psychic functioning. I fail to understand how observation and words as used in parapsychology can be a concept to find evidence of an afterlife. My own study observes what has, over a long period of time, (centuries) been scientifically written and reported. And, why I feel as a medium, I need to publish my own hypothesis on the 'testing of mediums'. Especially since numerous mediums from all over world have had evidence from the 'dead' repeatedly validated. As members of the general public we are led to believe the results of scientific studies on mediums to be always right, but based on what theory? Why is the demonstration of a communication from the 'dead' by a medium never right? The fallacy of science can in some cases determine the 'dead' do not exist.

In finding a few arguments in the area of 'testing mediums' I came up with a few opinions of my own. Usually arguments are written into journals or papers, but I will use an opportunity here in the next few pages.

Perhaps it's me and my view on parapsychology, but I find the 'testing of mediums' is a bit like going down the local pub and participating in a Quiz Night. The answers will always be a 'hit' or 'miss', right or wrong scenario. I see the similarities when mediums give information from the 'dead', the answers will always be a 'hit' or 'miss' ratio under scientific testing. The answers are words; words in my view cannot be seen and are not a science.

As a genuine medium I am interested in answers to questions that have not yet been found in the field of paranormal research. If you're like me, you probably want answers to questions too. Especially answers to questions relating to finding evidence of the soul's survival, or lack of it. I am interested as to why psychics, mediums and individuals who have extraordinary talent are constantly ridiculed and challenged about a belief system that has not been scientifically disproved.

The paranormal is a subject that has been of scientific interest for hundreds of years. And, after hundreds of years of scientific experiments with mediums, there has still been no progress made to accept the theory of an afterlife. The scientific theory is far too complicated - rejecting it is an easier scientific option. Perhaps one of the main reasons is because research funding has been limited, therefore hindered quantitative and qualitative studies. There is also the possibility that some researchers in this area do not want an outcome that is different from their own ideology, or religious tenet.

Nevertheless, since the subject is of public interest we could be made better aware of the 'hidden' science that is being written and reported on mediums and paranormal science. Science that is not readily available in the domain for public or 'open' discussion. The majority of that which has been written by scientists is within the constraints of scientific journals and papers. No one actually gets to see what's going on unless you know where to look for it. Should anyone be interested in it that is? If information was more widely available for perusal and discussion then perhaps we could all contribute our knowledge and experience more readily, given that, of course, mediums and those with a psychic talent are taken more seriously. Unless the whole functionalism of paranormal studies within academia is restructured and taken more seriously, we may never prove that there is something more than the life we now live.

Papers, journals and information written by scientists have given me the opportunity to raise my own arguments for discussion. It is only an argument, and one person's ideology may not be the same as the next person's, but it doesn't mean to say it doesn't exist. Besides, at any point in time it could be argued that any discipline claiming a scientific view, will have a current research paradigm. That is, a body of knowledge that is largely recognised by the research community and is considered an adequate explanation of the subject(s). Most research tends to reinforce the current paradigm, but typically, as more evidence accumulates about the paradigm's inapplicability, the more alternatives are proposed. These alternatives come from potentially bewildering and large set of choices, which can be loosely be classified fashionable to unfashionable.

Unsurprisingly, the new paradigm to emerge successfully to challenge the old paradigm tends to come from the fashionable end of the spectrum. Mediums and the spirit world have had a consistently bad press throughout history, leaving them at all times as an unfashionable paradigm alternative. This self-reinforces the idea that such a world is not scientific, or even that it is all imaginary. The fact that the only evidence accumulated over centuries indicates that there is some phenomena worth exploring and researching can be ignored if everyone agrees with its blanket condemnation. So the myth is sustained. After all, it's risky enough challenging any paradigm, but to suggest that the rigorous science of the current paradigm should be replaced with mediums and spirits cannot be seen in the current climate as helping with career progression!

However, fashion aside, my arguments exist when mediums are scientifically tested to demonstrate evidence of an afterlife. In many scientific studies the findings will argue 'no evidence was found to validate a mediums *claim* to communicate with the dead'. Naturally, I doubt if any medium would argue their ability to 'communicate with the dead'. A large population of mediums would support this claim.

But, is the area of parapsychology really about finding evidence of an 'after life' and the survival of consciousness, or is it about implications for other aspects of psychology? Are researchers in parapsychology demonstrating their results towards the 'testing of mediums', or are the results directed more towards implications relating to *neuropsychology*, as some would claim? Because the way I see it is, if evidence of the survival of physical bodily death and mediumistic abilities were valid, it would be a key challenge for *neuropsychological* research, would it not? Any evidence supporting the survival of bodily death would present allowances for parapsychologists to address and remodel their key assumptions, would it not? And, would it not allow for up-to-date research processes to be introduced according to modern day science? If the areas of psychology require more research, then so be it. We cannot deny the 'dead' exist because of any research 'implications'.

I have found in published papers that the majority of psychic experiments and methodology has not changed over the centuries. There is still the 'hit' and 'miss' ratio. The 'hit' and 'miss' ratio makes up a large part of a parapsychologists experiment in testing mediums. This hypothesis is used when a medium does well and the results, according to the researcher, are associated more with 'psychological stratagems'. In other words, guesswork has been used rather than a communication from the 'dead'. Probably an excellent ideology when a researcher cannot scientifically explain a medium's high 'hit' ratio. In my opinion, the idiom of 'psychological stratagems' is a conceptually false hypothesis when used to analyse messages received through spiritual communications. Moreover, a spiritual communication is not considered to be a psychological phenomenon, therefore, in reality, has no means of being scientifically measured.

The areas of 'generalisation' in statements appear to be very widespread amongst researchers. Yet, the majority of communications received by the medium form a basis of identifying a person, whether 'dead' or alive. In my view, a medium tested by a parapsychologist serves no purpose, since anything they say would purport to be 'guess work', or predominantly 'general'.

An example of hypothetical statements referred to as 'general' and to which often appears in research, and to which could purport to 'psychological stratagems', could be along the lines of when the medium acknowledges a young man in spirit. If the 'sitter' (person receiving a spiritual reading) was under the age of twenty, the word 'young' could relate to a grown child, teenager or someone who passed away in their late thirties. However, the latter would in comparison to the age of the 'sitter' not be young. Besides, can you interpret thirty as being young or old age? If a 'sitter' is only in their twenties, would they think of someone in their thirties as being young? Or, would they perhaps think 'thirty' to be 'older' than their own age? If the analysis of this hypothetical statement was psychologically analysed would the 'sitter' score higher by accepting the age range as being older than them? Can this type of hypothetical statement really and truthfully be accurately analysed?

Another type of 'psychological stratagem' that comes up in experiments is the amount of times a particular name is given by the medium. So, when in an experiment a medium receives the name of 'Jack' from a deceased person it becomes questionable. It becomes questionable because it is a name that is frequently given. Perhaps this is because, *'For the 11th year running Jack was the most popular newborn boy's name in 2005',* (Guardian, 2005). I'm sure many of us had a 'granddad Jack', an 'uncle Jack' or 'father' or 'brother' named 'Jack'. If you did then will someone explain to me as to why researchers feel cheated when 'Jack' is genuinely given as a name of a deceased person?

'Jack' will not be the only frequently given name either, as a portion of the 'dead' make up the names of Tom, Dick or Harry too. Suggestive statements by the researchers who refer to the possibility of a commonly used name as 'Jack' do not enhance the purpose of any scientific experiment. As such, the experiment would be open to suggestion from the researcher rather than the evidence. Would it not?

In my view, statements such as these present a good argument surely? For a medium to give any other name than that which is spiritually given would theoretically serve no purpose in experiments, except criticism. It is only when you associate a name with other information that a sitter can identify with that the message from spirit becomes evident. Identification and evidence of who I am for instance, is by the name I was given. I wouldn't want it changed to suit the hypothesis of a researcher. Additionally, 'general' statements could apply if a person had a beard, moustache, thinning hair, long hair, short hair and so forth. These types of people exist whether 'dead' or 'alive', so, can someone tell me why shouldn't this form of identification be given? Why is it if you give any of these attributes they are seen as 'general'? Would it be correct for a medium to describe a deceased person with a bald head then tell the sitter the man has a head full of curly hair? Absolutely not!

The deceased can also give a medium physical attributes associated with them, such as commonalities in scars, false teeth, ear piercings etc. So, when a medium is given one or more of these descriptions and analysed as a statement, the statement would be termed as 'general' in psychology. Statements such as these may be quite typical in many scientific studies, but in my opinion, if someone on the other side has a scar, false teeth or ear piercings, then the information should not be changed to indicate otherwise. I would consider any reference to a physical feature as being an accurate statement. Besides, hypothetically, a scar is a scar, you either have one or you don't, 'dead' or 'alive'.

When results in scientific experiments indicate 'no evidence was found to support or demonstrate either paranormal or mediumistic ability', I always feel quite biased. I am usually led to believe insufficient evidence was found by the researcher to suggest mediums were not able to demonstrate the presence of a deceased.

It is my view, parapsychologists and those with psychic abilities live in two very different worlds which do not fit one another. In comparison, my view of parapsychology does not fit into my world, nor does my psychic functioning fit into the world of parapsychology. Nevertheless, just because parapsychology does not fit into my world, or my view, it doesn't mean it is wrong. If my view could be supported by evidence accepted by parapsychology - psychologists would naturally change their view. Similarly, if parapsychology is supported by evidence accepted by me - I would change my view. No such evidence exists in the world of parapsychology since academic disciplines are a people who create ethical descriptions of the world which are neither proven nor unproven. But, it doesn't make it better than practitioners based on observation. Mediums are practitioners based on the subject they practice, more so than parapsychology since mediums interact with spirits and the 'dead'.

Since generalised statements have been well reported and written by scientists over the centuries, in my view current research fails to add anything new in methodology. It is because of the hypothesis in a range of psychological statements that invalidated communications from the afterlife improbable. Since the statements were a hypothesis of what could be termed 'general', the probability of the message being received from a deceased person was insufficient evidence. Since evidence of this nature is insufficient, I would argue how much evidence is required outside of the deceased person giving their name, identification traits and events?

Individuals have an identity of their own where they are recognised by others, whether 'dead' or 'alive'. It is the identity of a 'younger' man, false teeth, ear piercings, the name 'Jack', body scars, etc. that can form an important piece of evidence given by the deceased person. It is in my opinion, not a generalised statement, but solid evidence.

Psychics and mediums have been widely and successfully used by the Police in solving cases. Some have been used to successfully find missing persons. The majority have been sought to bring peace and closure into a person's life through the loss of a loved one. By dismissing the level of productive services psychic functioning is able to offer, science is dismissing something bigger. In suggesting how to move on from current 'scientific' practices to real exploitation of psychic power, there is a need to step out from criticism and into positive development.

Going back to the 'bit in the middle' I feel is missing. Perhaps this can be best described as metaphysical and where "each state of manifestation will be constrained by its dimensionality. By 'state of manifestation' we refer to those such as the physical world with its three dimensional mode of length, breadth and width. Time is sometimes quotes, but is, in fact a general value created by the existence of the other form-indicating dimensions. Accepting the reality and existence of a psychic energy world, one's freedom to move within it is greater than that of the physical world. In brief, it possesses more dimensions and fewer constraints. Beyond the psychic we may postulate etheric, astral, mental and other dimensional environments. The greater (more dimensions) will enclose the lesser when viewed from an Absolute. If we could discover a way of changing one dimensional state to another, then we could move from one world to another: In this case, from the physical world to the psychic. As both states represent specialised fields of energy, the translation from one to the other, lies in the control and interaction of those states" I thank John J Williamson, Society of Metaphysicians for this contribution.

In my own summary of 'testing mediums' I fail to see what evidence could be produced where two different kind of peoples' assumptions, and two different kind of people's views do not fit. Yet, another observation to be made is that of our science, knowledge and understanding. Where does our science fit into our knowledge and understanding? I leave to you find the answer yourself.

Carole Bromley

A Belief System

Proof of the afterlife has been demonstrated through the mass of psychic evidence provided by those with a sixth sense for many centuries. During that time there have been those who tenaciously commit and model themselves as 'sceptics'. Sceptics as we know exist both inside and outside the field of academia. Nothing wrong with being a 'sceptic', it's quite a healthy career, but only if you are able to leave out defamation of people's religion, faith and belief system. Because that's what it is, isn't it, a belief system that belongs to an individual person; a belief system that holds an individual truth?

I have found my own proof and truth as an individual over the years. At six years old I was there to witness the visitation of the clown from the spirit world. At the same age I had an extraordinary ability to hear voices from the grave. Even at the age of eleven the voices were still haunting me. Someone in spirit knew she was not coming back; someone told me she wasn't coming back.

My experience with the voices and levitating objects on the night of my sister's passing was not an accident. I believe my sister was coming home to tell me she had died. Whoever it was talking to me from beyond the grave tried to warn me. I believe people who pass can communicate with us and tell us of their passing. But, I was too young and lacked the knowledge to know that the voices belonged to 'dead' people. I hadn't realised the voices were speaking the truth.

I lacked the knowledge to know that the 'dead' can come back. No one told me because no one wanted to know. My family certainly didn't want to know about 'dead' people. Besides, who would tell a child about 'dead' people? It's different today though, children are growing up to learn about ghosts, spirits and the 'dead'. Parents are more open minded than mine were when I was a child. I can't blame my parents though, I realise now how individual an experience this phenomenon is.

Disturbing as it may be, when you first see a ghost or are witness to a visitation from the 'dead', it can be daunting. When spirits of the 'dead' started to appear in front of me, I found it to be very disturbing, even frightening at first. Well, it is frightening isn't it? Anyone who witnesses their first ghost and denies it frightened them is probably kidding themselves. However, because of the constant visitations from the spirit world it was something I had to get used to.

The more I witnessed and experienced the 'dead', the more I learnt how to communicate with them. I treated them as I would treat my own family, and as I would treat any person. I treated them as though they were still a human being and an individual, except they weren't human, nor of physical matter. Spirits are individuals and nothing can take that concept away from them. I learned to recognise that each spirit has its own identity and individuality, just as we have ours. Seeing spirit is an individual and personal experience of something you either believe in, want to believe in, or don't. We all have a choice.

I have made my own choice and choose to work with spirit as they have chosen me to work with them. It doesn't matter that sometimes I can or can't communicate with the 'dead', what matters to me is *how* the 'dead' can communicate. For me, the fundamental nature of having the ability to use psychic functioning is not enough. I always want to know more. I always look for evidence, and I always question evidence. I make a good sceptic, even to myself. But, no matter how much I learn or how much evidence I gather, it still doesn't answer my own questions of how the 'dead' manage to function, from a scientific point of view that is. I know that perhaps I will never find the answer to this question. It is probably a question that will take many more centuries to explain, if we are to rely on the progression of science that is. All I know is that somewhere in the universe, on a dimension different to that of our own, our consciousness has the ability to survive. Humans have the ability to survive.

Surviving criticism for something I believe in has led to me to question the human rights of individuals who are part of a religion, faith or belief system. People are entitled to belong to a religion, faith or belief system. My faith and belief system as a Spiritualist is a recognised legal orthodox religion. Spiritualism, or being spiritual, doesn't necessarily dictate that you need to belong to its movement, or its religion to believe in its principles. Nor is it a doctrine confined solely to the Spiritualist church, or those who practice or demonstrate 'mediumship'. It is a Universal growing faith and belief system open and accepted by a huge population of people. Precisely how much of the population has experienced, or witnessed a form of paranormal phenomena is to my knowledge unknown. Neither it is something to my knowledge that has been scientifically measured or proven. But, given that a huge population of people have experienced something paranormal does not mean to say we are all 'frauds'.

Belief in the paranormal is, in today's society, a recognised, accepted, reported and unreported dogma. However, if a person does claim to have witnessed a paranormal phenomenon, it does not make them a spiritualist - neither does it make a person a 'fraud'. It merely provides evidence of witnessing something outside a scientifically unproven belief system. Experience of the paranormal will influence a person's belief system.

My own belief system began with the loss of my sister. It was my reason for wanting to communicate with the 'dead'; it could well be the same reason that other people want to communicate with their loved ones. I understand why people who have no experience in communicating with the 'dead' suddenly decide it's something they want to do. Perhaps like me, it's because they want to know how our loved ones are on the other side. We want to know if they are happy, but I feel most of all, we want that direct link with them ourselves. It's a closeness perhaps we feel we need that comes from our love for them and from our heart. I know it is for me.

Talking to the 'dead' is becoming increasingly popular and of huge public interest in today's society. People appear to be learning more about the 'dead', spiritualism, and the paranormal than ever before. Perhaps it's because of the constant growing interest from the press, media and broadcasting of television programmes. And, as trends of public interest of psychic and paranormal phenomena grow, the trend for new methodology, science and scientific researchers will grow.

The growth of scientists investigating psychic functioning is welcoming news. People are now more open and able to talk and discuss their own experiences with ghosts and the 'dead'. However, since there is a huge population of people who want to learn more, there must also be a reason. Perhaps science can explore that reason. It cannot be that millions of people are 'hallucinating' when they experience something strange. No person can try to convince anyone who has experienced the paranormal that it was a 'hallucination'.

I'm quite adamant that nothing I have witnessed was caused by hallucinating. I know too that what I do see is not due to the imbalance of any brain chemicals, as some would lead us to believe. If this was the case then surely millions of others would have the same imbalance too. I don't believe for one minute that millions of people are mad! Neither is it for me, or others like me to try to convince or prove to others there is an afterlife.

The battle is for our scientists to prove to those millions of people who believe the afterlife does not exist.

I wasn't always a 'Spiritualist', the faith grew on me; I made up my own mind what it is that I truly believe in. Designing myself to follow a faith or be part of a faith was neither here nor there, I had my faith. I do however believe I am part of some religion, faith and belief system that is shared amongst millions of others. I used to be a sceptic too but learnt never to dismiss anything that I couldn't understand, since anything is possible.

There was a time when I would call myself a 'sceptic', not believing in 'ghosts' or 'apparitions' or life after death. Death to me was once morbid and spooky, not something to talk about, but something I had a fear of. No one wants to die do they; no one wants to think about death and dying? But it's there, it's a concept built into our physical human system. It's a clock waiting to stop.

However, it wasn't until I had proof and evidence of seeing and talking to the 'dead' that my scepticism changed. I believe people's perceptions of ghosts and the survival of the soul in the afterlife can change. Witnessing a ghostly apparition, unable to explain paranormal events, and receiving afterlife communications are just some forms of evidence that can change a person's belief system.

Those who haven't witnessed a form of paranormal phenomena are called 'sceptics', people who are over judgemental of others. People who themselves have little or no understanding of the subject they are critics of. They model themselves as judges who pass sentence on those who don't share the same belief system, or the same theory as they do. Can sceptics have an open mind? I don't know, it's hard to measure, but just because a person has no proof it doesn't mean that it isn't true. When it comes to the paranormal, sceptics have their own belief system, as I have mine.

A belief system is something everyone is party to whether they know it or not. But, how can a belief system be explained? What is a belief system? What do people believe in? What do you believe in? Is society influenced by the words or actions of sceptics, scientists, religion, press, media and belief systems? Aren't people entitled to make their own mind up which belief system they choose to endorse? Aren't people allowed to demonstrate what they believe in without being criticised? Whether a person is within or outside the confines of a church the belief is still the same.

My belief system as a child was influenced by the faith of Christianity, a religion to which I was baptised into and authenticated by a piece of paper I possess. I haven't got a foggiest idea where the paper is. It is most probably somewhere tucked away in a cupboard or drawer, or even lost. Wherever it is, apparently it is not important or I would know where it is. Now I'm all grown up, I can make my own choices in life. Since deceased people chose to communicate with me, I now know what my belief system is. I also now realise how much Spiritualism as a religion is discriminated against by those who do not share the same belief. I don't mind people not sharing the same belief as me, after all, if I hadn't had proof of my belief through spiritual voices and visitations I would probably be as sceptical as the next person.

Nonetheless, I didn't realise exactly how much I, and others like me would be discriminated against for something we believe in. I used to feel ashamed of being the spiritual person I am because of all the denigration from sceptics and the like. I used to feel it may be safer practicing as a Christian, my given faith, but I can't because I don't understand the bible. Besides, the bible would not give me the same proof that I get from the 'dead'. But, I came to understand that talking to the 'dead' wasn't going to go away. I didn't want it to go away; it has helped me so much.

My belief in Spiritualism helped me cope with my health. I suffered years of never ending bouts of panic attacks. I would panic in crowded places. If I went to the supermarket I couldn't stay because I would panic and have to go home. I would panic so much that I couldn't eat proper meals. I ate soup for six months because of the attacks. Going to work was difficult and embarrassing, especially if I knew an attack was going to happen. Taking Prozac prescribed by my doctor helped the panic attacks, but didn't cure them. I remained in this state for a few years until I got totally fed up and to some extent annoyed with myself. It was only through learning about Spiritualism and spiritual healing that the attacks went.

Instead of reaching for a bottle of Prozac every morning I would say a prayer. I would say a prayer before I went to sleep. I would ask God to take away the panic attacks so I could live a normal life. I began to think positive. Weeks went by before I realised I hadn't been taking the Prozac. I had been too busy occupying my mind with something I needed to believe in.

Learning about the afterlife was the right thing for me to do. I cannot recommend this would work for everyone, nor would I recommend anyone to stop taking any form of medication. All I can say is that my new found belief system worked for me. God worked for me, my belief in the afterlife worked for me.

I also looked into other religions and faiths, but not in order to make a change in what I believe in, or what others believe in. Exploring other religions helped me to understand what it is other people have a belief in. This approach and the knowledge gained served a better purpose over that of ignorance.

I may not agree with some concepts and principals of religions, at the same time, I wouldn't ask religions to prove to me and others what it is they believe in, or why. I know that the system they have chosen to have a faith in is of their choice and of their belief. What separates spirituality from other religions is the paradigm of spiritual communications from the deceased. The undisputed knowledge that God's life, and our life, is eternal. Spirituality is the only religion that recognises the existence of after death communications from deceased souls. Spiritualism is the only faith and religion that provides evidence of life after death.

Suffice to say I am not alone in my belief. I'm not the only person who can talk to the 'dead', (reassuring). There are millions of others who believe the same as I do, and who can also talk to the 'dead'. Millions of people have seen a ghost and are pretty adamant about what they believe they witnessed. Millions of people know that someone they love has been close to them at some time. Yet, we're not all hallucinating as some would have us believe. How bizarre to believe millions of people who share the same experience, seeing something relating to a ghost and other phenomena, are hallucinating! I'd like to think they were experiencing.

Sceptics and scientists are somewhat in the minority in that they have never seen a ghost, or spoken to a 'dead' person, so it's only natural they have their own fixed belief system. Millions of people, the majority, have witnessed an unexplained event. So, in retrospect, how can millions of people be told by a minority they have not witnessed anything paranormal? Question the minority before they class you insane, but just in case, my white jacket is hanging up in my wardrobe, clean and neatly pressed!

Its funny how life turns out when people like me do what we believe is right; do what we do because our human instinct is to help people. Sometimes we never expect to do what we do, but when we do we get discriminated against. Why? You may believe there is no afterlife because you yourself are afraid of death and dying. Perhaps looking beyond the concept of death is not acceptable for some. If you are a disbeliever of the extension of life in another world then you most probably judge those who do believe. By judging others it becomes a battle.

Yet, those who believe in the afterlife do not judge others as harshly or as critically, nor do they set out to destroy the belief system of others outside of their own ideology. Setting out to deliberately destroy a person's belief system, no matter what knowledge or evidence is lacking, does not qualify anyone to condemn or act as judge and jury. Spirituality is free will and an open house where everyone is welcome and anyone not excluded.

Belief systems can play an important part in the human race, an important concept to people's lives, identity and social culture. Spirituality is a belief system within a culture of millions, it deserves to be treated with a wider acceptance and understanding. Spirituality as a religion, faith and belief system has created a universal battlefield in its functionality and identity. Recent and past government petitions against fraudulent activity in the concept of mediumship are linked to those who hold a different belief system to that of Spirituality.

Spiritualism was officially recognised as an orthodox religion by a formal Act of Parliament in 1954. It is an act that appears to be unprotected from people lodging complaints and petitions to the Houses of Parliament. How many other people lodge complaints and petitions about other religions to the Houses of Parliament? Sadly for Spiritualists, they have to accept criticism of their orthodox belief system. In comparison to other religions, Spiritualism is the only religion open to state prosecution.

The 'Fraudulent Mediums' act was repealed in 1951, and again more recently because it was not a belief system recognised and supported by a certain population of people. Yet, it is still a belief system for those who choose to accept Spiritualism. Receiving communications from the 'dead' is a belief system for a majority of people. Whether a person is a spiritualist or not the choice in believing is there. Accepting the belief or not is freewill, it's not a crime, neither is it criminal. Belonging to any religious tenet is not criminal so why is Spiritualism any different?

It's funny how some of those in the world of academia can hold public seminars and lectures to demonstrate the 'dead' don't exist and charge a fee. Yet, is their demonstration any different to that of Mediums who equally charge a fee to publicly demonstrate the 'dead' do exist?

Mediums now have no choice but to accept communications from the 'dead' are for 'entertainment' or 'scientific' purposes only. Can you imagine someone you love contacting you through a medium for the purpose of 'entertainment'? Imagine being told that you have witnessed the appearance of a loved one purely for the 'purpose of entertainment'. Isn't the concept just a little bit disgusting? Isn't 'entertainment for the purpose of 'amusement'? Isn't amusement for the purpose of having a good laugh?

What's so amusing or entertaining about loved ones from the other side communicating with us? Those who work for the purpose of 'entertainment' are a critic to their own belief system. Those who work for 'scientific' purposes are wasting their time too, if science is what we are encouraged to believe.

You really do have to keep thinking spirit were once human. They are not aliens; neither are they guinea pigs or rats to be used in laboratories. They are of us, the 'Living Spirit'. They are our loved ones, family and friends, they are not for 'entertainment', nor scientific experiments. I sit on the fence with the best of them who have so far proved the same as me to some people, either nothing, or better still, more of nothing to the people who know nothing.

Conversations with the Dead

The process of the death of someone close, when it happens, is very difficult to cope with. When it does happen, we find we are thrown or drawn into the ambience of the sombre experience. Believe me, it is an experience and it is an extremely sombre occasion. We can have little understanding of just exactly how we can be affected when those who we love, or know, pass to the other side. No matter how many people close to us cross into the spirit world, the experience of death never gets any easier. In fact, it gets harder.

I know how much hardship death can cause. For me, death began with the loss of my sister, Christine. This was followed a few years later by the process of how death came to my step dad when he died from lung cancer. I would be at the bottom of the stairs in our house picking him up as he stumbled and fell. When my biological dad was admitted to Casualty I had to endure the sadness and tears of his terminal illness, he too had lung cancer. I would visit my dad in hospital for many weeks sitting at his bedside wondering what to talk about. How do you converse with a parent who is dying? How do you talk to someone to whom you are born to and who is dying? How do you look them in the face and tell them 'it's going to be ok' when it isn't? There's not a thing you can do, nor can they. I would hold Dad's hand hoping and praying he would get better when I knew he wouldn't. I felt useless.

The only comfort I could offer Dad was to talk about Angels. I prayed for the Angels to be by his side. I prayed for the Angels to help him cross over when he was called. I was pleased at first he didn't understand about me talking to the 'dead'. He would never talk about my work with spirit, until he began to realise he couldn't fight his disease and there was no way out of his condition. He would ask me questions about who I talk to in the spirit world, and if he knew anyone I spoke to. I knew he was afraid. I would always answer his questions truthfully; I couldn't make anything up nor would I want to, it's not something I do. After our talks I would leave his bedside with tears streaming down my face wanting his pain to end, wanting him to get up and walk out with me. I wanted my dad to live, except he wasn't going to get up, or walk out, at least not on his own. He spent the remainder of his last few weeks at home since it was his choice not to stay in hospital any longer than he 'needed'. There was no 'need' since there was nothing more that could be done.

Death is what we face and something we all can find extremely hard to come to terms with. There is no escape, no reprieve and no putting it off. There are no trial runs or any training. There is no 'if' there is only 'when'. The 'when' is something neither you nor I can prepare for. In a previous chapter, I told how I lost Mum to a heart attack and how I had not said all the things I wanted to say. I never said them because I didn't know she was going anywhere. I didn't know she would drop dead, Mum was supposed to be there for me. I always thought I would have plenty of time to tell her and show her how much I loved her. I never found the time, I was always too busy getting stuck into investigation reports and keeping up with my 9-5 job. Later always seemed to be a good time, big mistake, later never came.

Mum's passing was a shock and it was sudden. I had lived with her for the best part of thirty years. I wasn't prepared for her passing. When those we love go to heaven we are never prepared for their departure, this is what makes loving and appreciating everyone you love all the more important now, not later. Later may be too late! It is only later when the realisation of who and what you have lost happens. You never get over a loss, never, ever, never. When a loved one passes over to spirit the grieving process starts, it never ends. Whilst we are saying our final goodbyes to our loved ones, the spirit world is saying 'hello' and 'welcome back' to those who have just died. A new soul will be escorted over to heaven and welcomed into the spirit world by family who have gone before.

We are welcomed into the spirit world by members of our family who have gone before us. For me personally, I have felt real comfort knowing my family, who have gone before me, have been lovingly led over by my other family members to the spirit world. It's only when a deceased person adapts to the new conditions that they find they have the best of both worlds. There are no restrictions or visiting rights, they can come and go as they please.

My sister Christine invited me to her home in the spirit world on one occasion when she came to me through a dream. In the dream she was living in a magnificent huge and spacious glass house, complete with glass roof. Everything inside the house was pure white, clean, tidy and very spacious. I thought I was in the wrong house - she would laugh at that! I made a note to tidy up and wash the paint work down the next day in my own home! She made me a nice cup of tea and we sat chatting. It was some time before she led me outside into the grounds of her home. I was in complete admiration at how vibrant and blue the sky was with fluffy pure white clouds. I now know why the sky above us is called heaven. Yet heaven can be anywhere we want it to be.

My sister led me into a garden where my mum's clean white pet poodle played amongst the vibrant green bushes. This reminded me to call the groomer's for my dirty (white) looking west highland terrier! In front of me and all around me I could see rows of glass houses lined all along one side of the street. No house was joined to another and I stood looking at the incredible amount of space between each home. I embraced the magnitude and perfection of beauty before me. The sun shone gloriously over the green grass and neatly kept lawns. I reminded myself to tell hubby to mow the grass too when I got home. The winding roads were wide and made of tarmac just as they are here. I didn't see any other vehicles apart from the one I travelled home in. There was no one else around, just me, my sister and our dog; it was simply a place of perfection, a place known as heaven. I didn't want to leave but when it was time for me to go Christine walked me to a car that was waiting outside her house. I woke up smiling knowing she was still alive, very happy and very much a 'Living Spirit'.

I've always held onto that dream and I know there will be more opportunities to come, so long as I hold onto my love for her. But, I know it hurts, it hurts us all wanting to talk to someone we love that is no longer physically with us, wanting to talk to someone we love, but who has now died. It hurts not being able to see, hear, feel or hug them. Words cannot describe how it hurt me to lose both my parents and sister. It hurt that they had died because there were so many memories of them left behind, memories they had left me to remember them by. Except, I know none of them died really, I know where they are. They are in a place called 'heaven', happy, safe and at peace.

I will never forget Christine and I know although she is not here, she is still my sister. I remember one very special night when I had a visitation from her. I was woken up from sleep to find a mini Christmas tree by the side of my bed. The tree had twinkling lights and was floating in mid air. I knew it was Christine and knew that she was reminding me it was her. I smiled as I reached out and touched the tree. As I pulled my hand away a branch came with it. I felt a sense of peace knowing she was with me. I cried tears of happiness knowing my sister had given a piece of herself to me from the spirit world. I felt a sense of relief knowing my sister was still 'living' but not in the same world or the same way as I live.

It took me a long time to learn they lived on. Well, since the age of eleven anyway. It took a long time to believe they could exist somewhere close to me. And somewhere, I exist close to them. I know my sister hasn't died, never died, and couldn't die. I know she and I still share sisterly love. My sister loves to joke and play around, but she also has a serious side to her too. We share a love that is possible through our memories. Yet, it is more than a memory that allows her to communicate with me from the other side, and I her. Don't ask me how it is possible, I only know that it is. All I can say is thank God that possibility is there.

Like my sister, my mum and dad can also contact me. They have the ability to contact whoever they choose. Often they do. There is absolutely nothing shameful in keeping a deceased loved one's memory alive. Neither is it shameful to hold quiet conversations with them or any deceased pets. I do. I hold conversations with my parents, grandparents, pets and sister on a daily basis. I know Mum, bless her would miss our conversations if I didn't chat to her. Mum loved talking to people; she still does and will talk to me from beyond the grave.

I can always feel my sisters energy blend with my own. I can hear her voice when she talks to me. I can hear Mum's too when she nags me! I have never stopped loving any of them. That's why, for me, nothing is strange about wanting to talk to my loved ones on the other side. They don't die, we don't die. If you truly feel love for someone who has crossed over, that bond of love is not going to loosen. The memory of someone born to you, connected to you, or acquainted to you is not going to disappear. The memory of a deceased person's love lives on in many ways that is natural and normal. Just because a person isn't in a physically body doesn't mean they are not here, they are here. The only difference is that the 'dead' live on in a different shell to that of the physical body. The 'dead' are still a 'Living Spirit' in a dimension very close to me, you and everyone.

They come so close to us that sometimes it's hard not to notice they are with us. There are many signs that tell me when one of my loved ones are present. I can sense or feel one of them stand close to me. I don't have to ask who it is; I just know who it is. There may be times when I hear their voice talk to me, and I will talk back to them. At times when I feel I have been deserted I remind them I am still here. They never desert me. I know they hear me. There is nothing wrong with their senses, they function very well. And, just as we use our senses, spirit makes use of our senses too.

I find talking to my family and spirit comforting. If it comforts me by talking to them then it must be ok. I am always talking to them. I can't shut myself up once I start. Sometimes, I don't know who wants peace and quiet the most, me or them! A trip down memory lane and recalling all those beautiful memories can bring a feeling of comfort. As I tell everyone, all you need to do is sit back and talk to them as you would have when they were on the earth plane. Turn the telly off, have your moment and talk to those who you watch over you. They are a 'Living Spirit' too, let them guide you and continue to love you from the other side. Love them the same way you did when they were in the physical body. It works for me!

When I'm not working, a nice enlightening evening out for me, when time permits, is to go to a theatre to see a medium demonstrate 'conversations with the 'dead'. The abundance of love and sincerity whilst sat amongst others who believe brings a sense of pure love and peacefulness.

I always feel pleased when spirit manages to demonstrate their own personal skills by communicating through the medium. I am always pleased for the person who receives the communication. The atmosphere and energy the audience create is something that can be overwhelmingly felt, but only if you believe.

If you believe your loved one is close to you then keep believing. If you believe your loved one can hear you, keep talking and believing. If you believe you have heard a deceased loved one whisper your name, they did. If you believe your loved one can see you, they can. If you believe you have been helped by someone you love from the spirit world, it's probably because you have. If you believe conversations with the 'dead' has helped give you comfort, it did. Believe in those in the spirit world as they believe in you.

God Bless

Learning Lessons

Lessons on thought ...

- The mind is a very powerful tool.
- Everyone has the potential to develop their *sixth* sense.
- No one is too old to learn anything, anything is possible.
- You learn nothing without commitment and dedication. If you don't do the time your mind won't shine.
- Never expect anything to happen overnight, it very rarely does.
- If you want to be a professional medium, ask yourself why.
- Being a medium is about working with the 'dead'. Are you ready to talk to the 'dead'?
- Be prepared to learn the ability for flexibility.
- Every human being has their own DNA (Deoxyribonucleic acid), a blue print of cells that store information about our genetic make-up. Wherever we go we shed skin particles which hold our DNA. These particles are the component that carries residue energies that cannot be physically seen. These energies are can sometimes be that of which a medium can connect to.

On Spirit ...

- Spirit can be anywhere at any time.
- By opening up your mind to spirit – you are opening up to all spirits, positive and negative.
- A spirit is the conscious energy of a deceased person.
- Cases of a spirit or ghost physically harming a human being are very rare. It is not a spirit's intention to cause harm since they mostly work with an abundance of love.
- It's not a spirit that stays in any one place; it is the residue energy of the spirit. Often the energy of a spirit will move on.
- The spirit of our loved ones has the ability to make one or more visitations to the earth plane. Usually our loved ones will make frequent visits if we have an abundance of love that connects us to them.
- Spirits are born on the earth plane and have a human genetic connection. They are of someone's Mother, Father, Son, Daughter, Brother, Sister, Uncle, Auntie, Grandmother, Grandfather, Niece or Nephew. I tell you this because it may

be easier to relate to them the same way you would relate to members of your family.

- Spirits are not energies to be scared of. You are more likely to be scared of another human being than you are of a spirit.
- You don't contact spirit, they contact you.
- Spirits can be communicated with. Talk to them the same way you would talk to the 'living'.
- Spirits are highly evolved beings, they can help you.

On Ghosts …

- A ghost can be transparent in nature taking on the form of a physical body in whole or in part. Usually its appearance is transparent and grey but can also appear in colour. Sometimes this type of energy can appear in the form of a shadow. When a ghost is seen it can be similar to watching a re-play of an old film. A ghost is the energy of a deceased person that has the ability to manifest at any given time in any time period.
- Don't be afraid of a ghost and never show fear.
- A ghost was once a physical human being.
- The spirit of a ghost remains earthbound because it is trapped between the earth plane and another dimension. A ghost can also remain on the earth through a connection to a building. If a person loved a particular building or home then it would difficult for that person to leave, especially if it had resided in the same place for many years. Additionally, if a spirit had a great love for someone it would be heart-breaking for that spirit to leave. Sometimes, the spirit of a ghost is not aware they are 'dead'. This can happen when a person meets with a sudden and tragic ending to their physical life.
- The sighting of a ghost is validation of a haunting. Other signs of a ghost are associated with; flickering lights; mysterious audible sounds; unexplainable smells; feeling you're not alone but sense someone else with you; ethereal voices; shadowy figures ranging from transparent to solid matter. Sometimes the volume on a television or radio will increase/decrease. Electrical appliances will stop or malfunction for reasons that cannot be explained.
- The best thing to do when you *know* you are sure you have a ghost is ask them to leave. If you're nervous about doing this it may help to think of a friend who has outstayed their welcome and you want them to go. Ask a ghost who is visiting to leave the same way as you would ask a friend.

- There are many mediums that rescue ghosts and cross them over into the white light. If you can't find a reputable medium try your local Spiritualist church.
- Domestic ghosts are usually quite friendly and often related to occupants of the home or building.
- The moving of objects can occur if a ghost is distressed. The same happens with humans when they are angry, there may be the throwing or slamming down of objects under duress. Moving the spirit of the ghost into the white light, or asking it to stop or leave usually works.
- There are a variety of simple methods that can be used to find out if you are haunted: a) Voice recording equipment b) Thermometer c) Video equipment d) trigger objects e) photographs. The best time to investigate ghost visitations is during the course of the night when atmospheric energies are calmer and undisturbed.
- A spirit and a ghost have the ability to use all its senses, the same as we have the ability to use ours.
- Treat ghosts with respect.

On Spirit Guides ...

- We all have a spirit guide.
- We have one 'main' spirit guide who will work with us, should we be interested and remain with us throughout our earthly life before we exit the earth plane.
- We can have more than one spirit guide to help us on our earthly journey. Whenever our quest for learning different things change, so does another guide step forward to help us.
- New spirit guides will always work hand in hand with your 'main' guide.
- Your 'main' guide is always with you.
- People often think their guide has done a disappearing act, but this is not the case. There are times when people think because nothing is happening their spirit guide is not close by. Not true, and keep working with your guide whether you feel their energy or not.
- Spirit guides, like humans need to replenish depleted energy.
- Never assume spirit guides are with you 24/7.
- Permission can be given to your spirit guide to access your thoughts 24/7.
- The more you work with your spirit guide the more you can attune to the same pattern of vibration.

- Never shout at your spirit guide, they have ears and can hear you very clearly. The same goes for repeating things, it's not necessary. If you ask your spirit guide for advice, allow the energies time to work. Your guide is not a magician!
- Never assume your spirit guide will protect you from negative energies, or negative entities. Psychic protection is something you have to create and work with yourself.
- When your psychic sense of seeing opens and allows you to see spirit clearly, never assume the first spirit is your spirit guide. You may see many spirits and it may be that none of them are your guide.
- Spirit guides can appear surrounded by a glow of bright white light. They can also appear in the form of a glowing orb (energy of a spirit), or a light anomaly. Some spirit guides may not make an appearance at all. Of course, there are other forms a guide can make an appearance, you have to find out how by yourself.
- Getting started in communicating with your spirit guide is always best through regular meditation. There are many ways to work with your spirit guide. However, dedication, commitment, being truthful and finding time are important if you are to take working with spirit on a serious level.
- You have a right to question any information given to you by your spirit guide. From my own experience it pays to accept what you are told. However, there is no harm in testing your spirit guide, they will test you.
- Your spirit guide will help others who visit you when you are working.
- A spirit guide will never hurt or harm you. They work with complete love and divine light from the creator (God). You should work the same way.
- Enjoy your relationship with your spirit guide.

On Psychic Energies ...
- Sound waves travel through the universe and the ether. We know ourselves when we shout across a crowded room the sound we give out will be heard by someone. Because spirits have the ability to transmit messages, these message vibrations will also travel. Many people will have experienced hearing a voice, or being called by their name when no one is there.
- It takes a lot of energy for a spirit to communicate. It takes even more energy for a less experienced spirit to make a communication. Sometimes, if a spirit lacks sufficient energy, a

message being transmitted may appear distorted. It's a bit like a radio transmitter, if the airwaves experience interference you won't get to hear the complete song.

- Spirit energies have the ability to travel using portals. Portals are a gateway within the universe and the earth plane.
- Weather conditions can affect spirit communication. If a storm is taking place it may interfere with the frequency. Any adverse weather can interrupt a spiritual communication; this is because airborne particles and energies within the atmosphere are being moved around.
- Both negative and positive energies in the 'living' and the 'dead' can create a like-for-like attraction.

On Psychic Protection ...

- All spiritual work requires a level of psychic protection.
- The psychic protection force field is used to protect yourself from negative energies or spirits.
- Wherever you go make sure you visualise your bubble of white light protection. All negative energies, whether physical or psychic can be protected with the use of the psychic force field.
- Remember the psychic force field protection bubble first thing in the morning and last thing at night.

On Relaxation and Meditation ...

- Discipline yourself to meditate for 10 minutes every day.
- Use a timer to help monitor your time.
- Extend your time plan to 20 minutes once you get used to relaxing your body.
- Remember to use the psychic force field protection bubble.
- Try not to fall asleep.
- You will know when you are ready to meditate and connect with your spirit guide when you can a) stay awake, b) control your mind to focus.
- Ask 'yes' or 'no' questions. Keep questions short.
- Listen for a voice.
- Remember any images that are transferred to your mind.
- Take time to steady yourself fully after completing a meditation before moving. It helps to drink a glass of water straight after.

- Practice talking to your spirit guide regularly.
- Learn the art of patience; communications will be easy over time.
- Trust your spirit guide.
- Have confidence in what you are being told.
- Never doubt.
- Always say a thank you for information or spiritual guidance received. Even after working.
- Enjoy your meditation.

On Belief Systems ...

- Belief systems are personal and individual.
- Don't let others put you off your faith, belief system or religion as a spiritualist.
- You have nothing to prove to anyone but yourself.
- Accept that others may have a different belief system to that of your own.

On Communicating with Loved Ones ...

- Talking to your loved one doesn't hurt you or them, they enjoy being remembered and acknowledged.
- Many people talk to their loved ones on the other side; it's nothing to be ashamed of.
- Your loved ones can hear you and feel you.
- If you don't know what to say to them; talk about what you would have when they were here.
- Look for the tell tale signs that signify your loved one is close. Usually songs played on radio, things that would happen when they were here, things people say your loved one would have said. Flickering lights, odours such as scents or tobacco. A feeling someone is touching your hair or gently brushing your face. A feeling of someone being in the same room as you, yet you are completely alone. Being drawn to a particular item in a supermarket or shop that only your loved one would have bought. Hearing your name being called. There are many signs that tell us our loved ones have returned and are looking after us. You yourself will know what that sign is.

On the Dead ...

- The 'dead' are able to survive because their consciousness lives on in the ether (atmosphere). The physical body has been discarded which allows the spirit to travel through time and space.
- There are no dead.
- There is only peace and happiness.
- They live on without pain.
- Their love is eternal.
- The deceased keep the same personality, they do not change.
- No physical conditions are taken with them. They are healed.
- They can and do walk amongst us.
- They will never be forgotten.
- Communicating with the living helps them to evolve.
- Keeping an eye on those left behind is what they do best.
- Guidance is what they give when guidance is needed.
- Freedom to wander anywhere in space and time.
- Can make an appearance on audio and visual equipment, including photos.
- They are close to God and the Angelic realm. God blesses those who bless others.

On the 'Others' ...

C.R.E.A.T.I.N.S

'Completely Reject Everything About The Unknown or Not-knowable' Society (CREATINS)

This Society has been set up for those people who prefer to handle the unknown and the not-knowable by pretending non-existence as opposed to rising to a research challenge.

Membership of the Society

Membership is automatic and compulsory for anyone falling within the remit of the name of the Society. Applications are not allowed, you either qualify or not. Similarly you cannot resign your membership, it will continue unless at some point in time you see sense.

Rules of the Society

- Common sense (completely absent).
- You don't understand what the Society is for (you are a member and resignation is not permitted).
- Rational man, science are what you do, and nothing else is permitted.
- Xenophobia Rules OK'.
- If you come across evidence that suggests something unexplained is occurring and you cannot measure or record it then – something unexplained is not happening.
- People who believe that something is happening which cannot be explained or is non-knowable are clearly either: Deluded, or Charlatans, or Fraudsters.
- Officers of the society cannot be members since their function is to make a nonsense work.

Membership Levels

There are 7 'easy' levels of membership:

1. Elite Membership is automatically awarded to those who believe this Society does not exist.
2. Everyday Member: if you find the idea of CREATINS laughable.
3. Exceptional Member: if the idea of CREATINS makes you angry.
4. Excellent Member: if you try to argue for the suppression of CREATINS.
5. Exemplary Member: if you seek legal redress about your membership.
6. Exalted Member: if you can get your views published in the academic literature.
7. Eccentric Member: if you are proud to be a member.
   Ray J Paul

Free Spirit

I hold your photo in my hands
A memory of your life so grand
I see your face that watches me
In my heart I know you're free
No pain or sufferings have you now
For you have taken your last bow

I know the place where you now rest
For it is Seven Archangels Crest
I know your voice I will always hear
Your presence I will never fear
I'll wait for you to contact me
A living spirit we both be

I hold your photo in my hands
I know it's hard to understand
I cannot see you next to me
But I feel your love is close to me

Please my darling don't leave me
But use your thoughts to speak to me
I know you are but a step away
A shining light of God's delight

Copyright of Carole Bromley

My views I have expressed in some chapters are entirely my own views and without prejudice to anyone, or any professional body. Many of the names used are of real people but have been changed to protect their privacy.

To my friends, family and colleagues who have given me encouragement and inspiration. I thank Ioannis, Nav, Nayna, Steve, Anastasia, for all the help given me in trying to find my own words. I'd like to further acknowledge my investigation team members; Agnes, Rob, John, Pablo, Beth, Glenda, Steve, Terry, Mark for their hard work, dedication and commitment given to all the investigations we have undertaken.

My friends Elaine, Carole, Heather, Lesley, Jan, Debbie, Lorraine, Julie, Bev, Den, Jacky, Jasna, Kay, Sandra, Tracey, Chris, Jo, Roxanne, Sheena, Angela, Daryl, Den, Lesley-Ann, Lampros, Panos, Natasha, Monica, Krista, Joe, Pol, Marjie, Mary, Hazel, Dawn, Charlie, Sue for their kindness, encouragement and friendship. My thanks also to Agnes for her inspiration, and to my dear departed friend and colleague Marion Smith. Finally, thanks to Jackie Weaver, 'The Animal Psychic' for helping to republish my 2nd edition of this book. Ron Bowers for the cover photo (copyright). My love and appreciation to you all.

The battle continues!

Glossary of Terms

Clairaudience: A person who has a clear psychic sense of hearing.

Clairvoyance: A person who has the ability to obtain information, or see spirit and visions clearly.

EMF: Electro Magnetic Field Meter used to measure fluctuations of electromagnetic energy.

Entity: Supernatural being.

Ghosts: A deceased person's disembodied spirit which can often be seen as an image being replayed on a film.

Haunted: Unexplained phenomenon.

Medium: An appropriate name for a person who acts as a translation link through spiritual contact.

ORB: A sphere of light that appears in photographs or other forms of recording images. Can also be seen with the naked eye and is usually known to be a symbol of the presence of a spiritual energy.

Parapsychologist: A Person who has a degree in the subject of psychology and uses it as an extension to research areas of the paranormal.

Psychic: Ability to perceive information by use of the sixth sense.

Psychic Protection: Visualisation of a white light used by the mind to protect oneself on a spiritual level.

Séance: A group of people who gather to communicate with spirit.

Spirit: Residue energies of the human consciousness left in the atmosphere after physical death.

Spirit of the Glass: This version of an improvised Ouija board is often used in a séance. Lexicon cards in alphabetical order are placed around a table to form a circle. Two cards with the words 'Yes' and 'No' are placed either side of the glass centred in the middle of the table. A person or persons place their index finger lightly on top of the glass to allow free-flow movement. When spirit contact is made the glass will move to spell out a word.

Trance: Spirit uses the vessel of a medium to use direct communication. There are many forms of trance practiced by mediums.

Transfiguration: When transfiguration takes place, features of the spirit entity can be seen superimposed over the face of the medium.

Trigger Objects: Small lightweight household objects used as experiments to enable spirit to identify their presence.

White Light: The white light is something people claim to see when experiencing a NDE (near death experience). The light has been described as a tunnel they have entered which when travelled through takes a person to the 'other side', or heaven. It is the same light that all spirits use to travel through, and all mediums visualise for the purpose of crossing over spirit.

References

Butt, R, Article Title: *'New old-fashioned' Jack is most popular name for 11th year*, (24 December 2005), Available at: http://www.guardian.co.uk/uk/2005/dec/24/britishidentity.uknews2, Accessed: April, 2008

Paul, Ray, J. (2006) *To Know or Not To Know, (2006)*

Paul, Paul, J, *C.R.E.A.T.I.N.S, (2008)*

Paul, Ray, J, Living with Parkinson's disease: Shake, Rattle & Roll. RAIL, London (2009

(ISBN: 978-0-9563145-0-5)

Terrill, C. (2005) *Inside the Royal Navy Today*, Shipmates, p.244

Williamson, J J, (2009)

www.carolebromley.com

www.metaphysicians.org.uk

Printed in Great Britain
by Amazon